Tourism, Sanctions and Boycotts

This is the first book to provide a comprehensive account of sanctions and boycotts in tourism and the economic and ethical complexities that policy makers, tourists, tourism destinations, and businesses face.

Sanctions and boycotts are an important feature of the global tourism system and the emerging ethics of tourism. Sanctions and embargoes are increasingly used as coercive instruments of diplomacy and foreign policy by the United Nations, supranational organizations, the US, and other nations to change the actions and behaviors of countries, organizations, businesses, and individuals. At the same time, boycotts and buycotts are a growing feature of political consumerism and interest group activism. Tourism and hospitality destinations, attractions, and businesses can be profoundly affected by this, with the legacy of a negative image lasting for decades. International travel to some destinations may be severely restricted, financial investment and supply chains disrupted, and, in the most comprehensive sanctions and boycotts, substantial economic and personal hardship may be experienced.

This book is of interest not only to policy makers, destination management and marketing organizations, and students of crisis and politics in tourism and hospitality but also those who seek to address the interrelationships between sanctions, tourism destinations and attractions, and the tourists who boycott them.

Siamak Seyfi is a lecturer in the Department of Tourism at the University of Pantheon-Sorbonne, France. Using primarily qualitative and mixed methods, his research interests focus on tourism politics and geopolitics, political ecology and tourism, power and the environment.

C. Michael Hall is Professor in the Department of Management, Marketing and Entrepreneurship at the University of Canterbury, New Zealand; Docent in Geography, University of Oulu, Finland; and Visiting Professor at Linnaeus University, Kalmar, Sweden. He has published widely on tourism, regional development, global environmental change, sustainability, food, and World Heritage.

Routledge Focus on Tourism and Hospitality

Routledge Focus on Tourism and Hospitality presents small books on big topics and how they intersect with the world of tourism and hospitality research. The idea is to fill the gap between journal article and book. This new short form series offers both established and early-career academics the flexibility to publish cutting-edge commentary on key areas of tourism and hospitality, topical issues, policy-focused research, analytical or theoretical innovations, a summary of the key players or short topics for specialized audiences in a succinct way.

World Heritage and Tourism
Marketing and Management
Bailey Ashton Adie

Tourism and Urban Regeneration
Processes Compressed in Time and Space
Alberto Amore

Tourism, Sanctions and Boycotts
Siamak Seyfi and C. Michael Hall

For more information about this series, please visit: www.routledge.com/tourism/series/FTH

Tourism, Sanctions and Boycotts

Siamak Seyfi and C. Michael Hall

LONDON AND NEW YORK

First published 2020
by Routledge
2 Park Square, Milton Park, Abingdon, Oxon OX14 4RN

and by Routledge
52 Vanderbilt Avenue, New York, NY 10017

Routledge is an imprint of the Taylor & Francis Group, an informa business

British Library Cataloguing-in-Publication Data
A catalogue record for this book is available from the British Library

Library of Congress Cataloging-in-Publication Data
A catalog record has been requested for this book

ISBN: 978-0-367-23282-5 (hbk)
ISBN: 978-0-429-27910-2 (ebk)

Typeset in Times New Roman
by Apex CoVantage, LLC

Contents

Figures

Tables

Boxes

Preface

To many, especially those concerned with promoting tourism and travel, tourism is seemingly about freedom of movement. However, the reality is vastly different, with millions of people around the world constrained because of wealth, gender, patriarchal societies, institutions, and politics. At a time of increased nationalism, demonization of the other, and efforts by some governments to deliberately dismantle the multilateral world order, the capacity to travel often appears more restricted than ever.

This book has been written to detail an increasingly important component of the politics of tourism. Sanctions are a tool of international geopolitics, the rights and wrongs of sanctions lie within shades of grey, and their success is often limited. However, many ordinary people suffer as a result, and it is with them that our sympathies lie. To us such understandings lie at the heart of any ethics of tourism and the way tourism and the tourism system are inseparable from political economy, something that many of our colleagues conveniently ignore. As such, tourism can shed considerable light on sanctions policies and their effects and vice versa.

The top-down efforts of sanctions to change country and organizational behaviors are contrasted in this book with the more bottom-up actions of boycotts and buycotts. Although multi-lateral based sanctions are often justified by an appeal to international norms, boycotts possess a stronger ethical grounding for action against countries, corporations. Indeed, in many cases boycotts occupy the ethical space that some governments, businesses, and leaders lack. They also point to new ways of understanding political consumerism in a tourism context and may also suggest some directions for ethical tourism purchase, especially when considering issues of climate change, the environment, and human rights. As such we hope that, if only in some small way, this short book contributes to a broader – and better – understanding of the politics and ethics of tourism.

Siamak would like to dedicate this book to the ordinary Iranian people who have encountered hardship as a result of sanctions: to the many Iranians who desperately search for medicine restricted by the sanctions, those who experience staggering prices and shortages, and to those who died in commercial airplane crashes because of the lack of pieces banned or restricted by sanctions.

Nobody has been more important to Siamak in the pursuit of this project than the members of his family. He would like to thank his parents and especially his late father whose love and guidance are with him in everything he pursues. He also wishes to thank his loving and supportive wife, Mina, for her enduring love and patience.

Michael would like to thank a number of colleagues with whom he has undertaken related conversations and research over the years. In particular, thanks go to Bailey Adie, Alberto Amore, Dorothee Bohn, Tim Coles, Hervé Corvellec, David Duval, Alexandra Gillespie, Martin Gren, Stefan Gössling, Johan Hultman, Dieter Müller, Paul Peeters, Girish Prayag, Yael Ram, Anna Laura Raschke, Jarkko Saarinen, Dan Scott, Anna Dóra Sæþórsdóttir, Allan Williams, and Maria José Zapata-Campos for their thoughts on tourism, as well as for the stimulation of Agnes Obel, Ann Brun, Beirut, Paul Buchanan, Nick Cave, Bruce Cockburn, Elvis Costello, Stephen Cummings, Chris Difford and Glenn Tilbrook, David Bowie, Ebba Fosberg, Aldous Harding, Father John Misty, Mark Hollis, Margaret Glaspy, Aimee Mann, Larkin Poe, Vinnie Reilly, Henry Rollins, Matthew Sweet, David Sylvian, and The Guardian, BBC6, JJ, and KCRW – for making the world much less confining. Special mention must also be given to the Malmö Saluhall, Balck and Postgarten in Kalmar, and Nicole Aignier and the Hotel Grüner Baum in Merzhausen. Finally, and most importantly, Michael would like to thank the Js and the Cs who stay at home and mind the farm.

We also wish to gratefully acknowledge the help and support of Jody Cowper for proofreading and editing. Finally, we would both like to thank Emma Travis, Lydia Kessell, and all at Routledge for their continuing support.

Abbreviations

CAPS	Companion Animal Protection Society
CSR	corporate social responsibility
ECRA	Ethical Consumer Research Association
FRYSM	Federal Republic of Yugoslavia (Serbia and Montenegro)
HFA	Humane Farming Association
ICJ	International Court of Justice
ILGA	International Lesbian, Gay, Bisexual, Trans, and Intersex Association
JCPOA	Joint Comprehensive Plan of Action
LGBT	lesbian, gay, bisexual, and transgender
MSF	misappropriation of state funds
OAPEC	Organization of Arab Petroleum Exporting Countries
OFAC	Office of Foreign Assets Control
OIC	Organization of Islamic Cooperation
OPHR	Olympic Project for Human Rights
PACBI	Palestinian Campaign for the Academic and Cultural Boycott of Israel
PETA	People for the Ethical Treatment of Animals
RFL	Religious Freedom Laws
SCO	Shanghai Cooperation Organization
SDN	Specially Designated National
TfL	Transport for London
UDHR	Universal Declaration of Human Rights
USOPC	United States Olympic and Paralympic Committee
VFR	visiting friends and relations
WEOG	Western European and Others Group
WMD	weapons of mass destruction

1   Introduction and context

Sanctions can be poorly conceived, and history reveals them to be a blunt tool for changing conduct. US measures taken against Cuba since 1960 did not produce regime change. The US and Europe imposed an arms embargo against China after the 1989 Tiananmen massacre which did little to improve the human rights situation in that country, or to prevent its military build-up – in part because the UK and France differed in their interpretation of the ban. But others did bring results. Apartheid in South Africa came undone in a context of international sanctions. Under Barack Obama, sanctions played a key role in getting Iran to the negotiating table. Penalties levied on Liberia helped precipitate the collapse of the presidency of Charles Taylor, who later stood trial for crimes against humanity for his actions as a warlord. Sanctions are also a much better option than military action.

Editorial, *The Guardian*, 6 August 2017 (The Guardian, 2017)

Introduction

The threat or the actuality of a sanction or boycott is daily news in contemporary media. Although they play a major role in international geopolitics, as the above quote from the editorial of *The Guardian* illustrates, their role as a factor in tourist behavior and tourism development has received far less coverage. Yet sanctions and boycotts are topics of significance to many tourism businesses and destinations either as a direct result of their impact or because they affect the image and the relative attractiveness of different competitors. In the latter case the impact of sanctions, for example, is not just because of their direct impacts on the capacity to travel and do business, exchange rates, and investment but also because they can substantially affect the perception of a destination in the eyes of consumers in tourist generating markets over the long-term. This first chapter provides an introduction to the topic of sanctions by giving a brief historical outline of their development as well as identifying some working definitions of sanctions and boycotts. The chapter then goes on to discuss the scope of some of the different levels of sanctions as well as their role within foreign policy and international relations.

Historical perspectives

The use of sanctions by a state against other states or parties has a long history and has been integral to the repertoire of coercive foreign policy measures for centuries (Hufbauer, Schott, Elliott, & Oeggm, 2008; Lopez & Cortright, 2018). The history of sanctions goes back at least to circa 432 BC, when the ancient Athenian statesman and general Pericles issued the so-called 'Megarian decree' in response to desecration of a sacred site and the abduction of three Aspaisan women and banned the Megarians from trading at Athenian markets (Hufbauer, Schott, & Elliott, 1990). However, the understanding of sanctions and their role and uses as a foreign policy implement and diplomatic tool has changed over time, shifting from being regarded as a component of warfare to one that is designed to prevent the need for military action and also target states or other actors that operate against international norms (Table 1.1). Although it is important to note

Table 1.1 Emergent trends in use of sanctions as a foreign policy tool

Sanctions focus	Period	Characteristics
Sanctions as an auxiliary feature of war	19th century and early 20th century to present	Loosely governed by customary international law on blockades, contraband, and rights of neutral states. Napoleon used economic sanctions on the United Kingdom, known as the continental system or blockade, to try to damage the UK economically while developing continental industry and trade.
Sanctions against aggression	1930s to present	Discussion surrounding the question of aggression in face of attacking and occupation of other countries by major powers and the positioning of the international community toward it (e.g. economic blockade of Germany in the aftermath of the First World War and its effectiveness due to the economic strains put on the Wilhelminian regime, sanctions against Japan's attack in 1931 on China and the following occupation of Manchuria and sanctions against Italy's war against Ethiopia.

Sanctions focus	Period	Characteristics
Sanctions for Decolonization	1960s	The second sanctions debate was concerned with issues of decolonization, discrimination, democratic rule / the adoption of sanctions as 'the economic weapon' by the UN Charter (e.g. UN comprehensive sanctions on South Africa and Southern Rhodesia) / Initiation of unilateral sanctions by major powers and outside the framework of the UN (e.g. sanctions on Cuba and the Dominican Republic (by the USA), on Albania and China (by the USSR), on Portugal, South Africa and Rhodesia (by Afro-Asian states)).
Sporting and cultural sanctions and state supported boycotts	Late 1960s to present	In part a continuation of sanctions for decolonization but also a response to the emergence of intermistic issues such as human rights. Best illustrated by Olympic and Commonwealth Games actions but also other sporting and cultural events and relations.
Sanctions and the New Wars	1990s to present	Focus of sanctions on territorial aggression and breaking peace / UN sanctions on Iraq (under Chapter VII) in the aftermath of Iraq's invasion against Kuwait / a record number of sanctions applications by the United Nations in the 1990s (e.g. Somalia, Liberia, Angola, Rwanda, Sierra Leone, and FR Yugoslavia (Kosovo)).
Targeted and Smart Sanctions	2000s to present	Evidence of the harmful effects of sanctions on vulnerable civilian groups and their collateral damage to third states (e.g. Iraq's sanctions regime) and the poor record of effectiveness of sanctions in achieving the predetermined objectives / improving the design and implementation of sanctions to reduce the collateral damage to the general population and third countries / growing emphasis on a policy alternative for targeted or smart sanctions though arms embargoes, travel bans, and asset freezes (e.g. the European Union 'blacklist' of 600 Serbian President Milosevic's supporters; the flight ban imposed on Libya; US bans on Taliban).

Sources: Adapted from Wallensteen (2000) and Hufbauer et al. (2008)

that the various developments in the uses of sanctions do not supplant each other over time but instead should be seen as additional dimensions to how sanctions are justified in diplomatic and foreign policy terms, with their use being actor and context dependent.

As Hufbauer (1998, p. 332) observes, in the first phase, 'From the Napoleonic wars through World War I, economic sanctions were almost entirely an auxiliary feature of war, loosely governed by customary international law on blockades, contraband, and rights of neutral states'. The continental blockade of the Napoleonic wars of 1803–1815, which forbade European nations from trading with the UK to cripple the United Kingdom economically was one of the earliest and most comprehensive attempts of imposing sanctions (Nicholson, 1967). Known as the continental system or blockade, the sanctions sought to try to damage the UK economically while developing continental industry and trade (Selden, 1999; Naylor, 2001). However, the blockade had only limited impacts on the UK economy with the UK increasing trade elsewhere in the world such as the Americas and Africa. The blockade also negatively affected some of the European countries, such as the Netherlands, leading to reduced support for Napoleon (Crouzet, 1964). During the Napoleonic period, the War of 1812, and until entry into World War One their use by the United States reflected international norms that narrowed the scope of definitions of contraband and enlarged the rights of neutrals, although during the Civil War the North took a much broader interpretation against the South (Hufbauer, 1998).

The modern application of sanctions can be seen in a number of economic sanctions imposed during and after World War 1, such as those advocated by President Woodrow Wilson of the United States, which sought to limit military aggression and the occupation of countries by major powers. In 1919 President Wilson argued, 'A nation that is boycotted is a nation that is in sight of surrender. Apply this economic, peaceful, silent, deadly remedy and there will be no need for force' (quoted in Hufbauer et al., 1990, p. 9). After World War I extensive attention was given to the notion that economic sanctions might substitute for armed hostilities as a stand-alone policy (Hufbauer et al., 2008). The enthusiasm for the use of economic sanctions (an 'economic weapon') rather than force (a 'military weapon') to make countries desist from aggressive acts dates from this time and has become a cornerstone of the positioning of the international community toward the imposition of sanctions that lingers to the present-day. In the inter-war period the League of Nations introduced the notion of internationally authorized sanctions in actions against Bolivia, Greece, and Paraguay as well as sanctions against Japan's attack in 1931 on China and sanctions against Italy in 1935 following Italy's war against Ethiopia. However, it was the failure of sanctions against Italy following their invasion of Ethiopia, primarily as a result of a failure to be able to restrict access to oil supplies, that substantially contributed to the demise of the League (Hufbauer, 1998). It should also be noted that US sanctions against Japan may have contributed to the Japanese attack on Pearl Harbor.

The US imposed sanctions on Imperial Japan in 1940–1941, culminating in an oil embargo and the seizure of Japanese assets in July 1941. The purpose of the sanctions was to deter Japan from invading Southeast Asia and persuading them to withdraw from Indochina and China. In response Saunders (2014) argued that Japan concluded that American sanctions made the occupation of Southeast Asia essential in order to access resources, especially oil, as well as the devastation of the United States Navy. Importantly, and reflecting the notion that sanctions are an auxiliary feature of war, Japanese leaders perceived little distinction existing between economic sanctions and warfare, and if sanctions would make their country weaker over time then it would be politically and economically prudent to strike sooner rather than later (Saunders, 2014).

After World War II, the United Nations sought to formalize a method of managing global security through its Security Council, and since then, it has managed to impose sanctions with varying degrees of success. Nonetheless, post-World War II, the UN Security Council's role in defending international norms was constrained by US-Soviet rivalry – in which economic sanctions and opportunities were widely used as a means of statecraft. The Cold War-era split that divided the world community into East, West, and the nonaligned substantially prevented the use of concerted worldwide action to meet humanitarian, peacekeeping, and human rights challenges and thereby forestall armed conflict (Lopez & Cortright, 2018). During this period UN members often failed in reaching a consensus on whether the actions or policies of a country threatened international peace and stability. And, even when they agreed on this, they did not necessarily agree that the imposition of sanctions was the best course of action (Rossignol, 1996). Many other factors were involved, including the 'reality of international relations where perceptions of delinquency can vary significantly and foreign – and domestic – policy considerations often rule out hostile action toward another state' (Doxey, 1990, p. 246). As a result, although representatives of various countries in the General Assembly of the United Nations often called for the imposition of sanctions, until the end of the Cold War action was seldom taken either because of a lack of consensus or because of a veto by the permanent members of the Security Council (Rossignol, 1996).

There were only two notable exceptions in the climate of Cold War politics. First, the imposition of sanctions in the form of arms embargo against the Smith regime in the former self-governing British Crown Colony of Southern Rhodesia (what is known as Zimbabwe today) in 1966 in response to the unilateral declaration of independence by white Rhodesians in 1965. This was the first mandatory arms embargo agreed by the UN Security Council. Second, sanctions against South Africa in 1977 following the eventual and nearly unanimous world condemnation of the racist apartheid regime. However, the South African and the Rhodesian cases also reflected broader international agreement in the use of sanctions to encourage decolonization, particularly in Africa. Such measures also brought about the use of state sanctioned boycotts of sporting and cultural arenas. For example, the 1986 Commonwealth Games in Edinburgh were substantially affected by the withdrawal of African, Asian, and West Indian competitors over UK Prime Minister Thatcher's policy on South Africa. The media attention given to the Games provided the boycotting countries an opportunity to attempt to pressure the British Government into altering its stand on relations with South Africa and therefore encourage the South African government to negotiate (Hall, 1992). This also reflects the notion that 'The main purpose of sanctions is not to punish white South Africa for the sins of apartheid, but rather to push it to the conference table to negotiate a hand-over of power to bring about majority rule and "one person one vote"' (Hanlon & Omond, 1987, p. 12).

The post-Cold War period has witnessed a sharp rise in sanctions imposed on countries with renewed state interest in their use as a foreign policy tool (Cortright & Lopez, 2018a). According to Farrall (2007) there are two factors that contributed to the rise of sanctions in the aftermath of the Cold War. First sanctions have come to be viewed as a lower-cost, lower-risk, middle option between diplomacy and war (Masters, 2017) and often represent 'the least unpalatable of the coercive alternatives available to the UN Security Council when faced with the task of taking action to maintain or restore international peace and security' (Farrall, 2007, p. 3). Farrall explains that:

> From a political perspective, it can be extremely difficult to garner the support necessary to authorize collective military action under Article 42 of the UN Charter, as the governments which would be expected to shoulder the burden of collective forceful action are reluctant to assume responsibility for the serious financial, political and humanitarian consequences that are likely to flow from the use of military sanctions. The imposition of non-military sanctions, by contrast, is generally thought to entail fewer costs than the use of force. By authorizing sanctions, the Security Council can be seen to be taking strong symbolic action against threats to international peace and security, without having to assume the responsibility for, or incur the costs of, using force.
>
> (2007, pp. 3–4)

Second, the effectiveness of sanctions in achieving the policy objectives is perceived to be largely increased with the progress in technology and communication and trade in a globalized world. Farrall explains that: 'Globalization has fostered a climate of growing interdependence, in which states are increasingly reliant upon trade and communication links with the international community. In such an interdependent economic environment, a stringent UN sanctions regime has the power to devastate a target economy and to rein in target political elites' (2007, p. 4). Such perspective harks back to the arguments of Woodrow Wilson at the end of the first World War in favor of economic sanctions.

'Sanctions, or the threat of their imposition, are successful to the extent that they contribute to promoting the change desired by those who imposed or support sanctions' (Crawford, 1999, p. 5). Yet, as discussed in this book, while they remain a popular policy tool they are often not successful in achieving their aims and may even have substantial unintended consequences. As Rossignol (1996) observed

> A country can resist sanctions for long periods, especially if their effectiveness is undermined by sanctions-busting and disagreements within the international community on how extensive they should be. Since sanctions cannot always produce the desired results, enthusiasm for using them as a coercive tool has ebbed and flowed in the decades since the First World War.

Nevertheless, they are an integral part of contemporary geopolitics and are a vital element of the political and business environment that surrounds contemporary tourism.

Definitions of sanctions

Although there is no standard definition of international sanction, they are usually defined in terms of state related foreign policy actions and are measures applied in relation to a perceived wrongdoing by a state, organization, individual, or other identified actor

> Sanctions usually consist of a ban on the sale and shipment of products to a country and on the purchase of its exports. Other elements not directly linked to trade and commerce, such as culture and sports, are now often included. Thus we see bans on economic, sporting and cultural contacts between countries, as well as "person-to-person" sanctions such as withholding visas or other diplomatic documents from citizens of another state.
>
> (Rossignol, 1996)

Crawford (1999), in an influential volume on the role of sanctions in apartheid South Africa, defined sanctions as:

> sanctions are defined as the denial of customary interactions (strategic, economic, or social); they are intended to promote social, political, or economic change in a target state. As the denial of customary interactions, sanctions speak louder than words: imposition of sanctions communicates the threat of more sanctions and also the promise of release from embargoes if the target meets certain conditions.
>
> (Crawford, 1999, p. 5)

Fundamentally, sanctions are intended to persuade the target actor to change actions or policies. A number of synonyms are also used for sanctions including: blockades, boycotts, embargoes, and are sometimes even described as quarantine or economic coercion. These concepts are almost synonymous (Wallensteen, 2000), although boycotts have increasingly come to be tied to consumer or collective individual actions although these may be state sanctioned and encouraged (see Chapter 3). In sanctions terminology, a distinction is also sometimes drawn between 'embargoes' and 'sanctions', with the former representing prohibitions against the export to the target of a particular product or commodity and the latter encompassing either the export to or the import from the target of particular products or commodities (Farrall, 2007).

The meaning of the term 'sanctions' can be different in different contexts. Table 1.2 compares the meaning of sanctions in the domestic and international spheres. In the domestic context, sanctions generally represent a range of action that can be taken against a person who has transgressed a legal norm and the nature, scope, and length of potential national sanctions are generally determined by legislatures (Farrall, 2007) (see Box 1.1 for an example of a potential domestic sanction). The fundamental difference between the domestic meaning of sanctions and the popular understanding of sanctions in the international context is that the action commonly referred to as sanctions in the international sphere does not necessarily serve the purpose of enforcing a legal norm and instead may be used for political and foreign policy purposes.

A further complicating element in understanding the definition and application of sanctions is that it is important to recognise that they do not just apply in the economic sphere, as significant as that is, or on a state basis. Although frequently referred to as boycotts (see Chapter 3) sanctions can also be undertaken by international and domestic organizations, alliances, corporations, universities, municipalities, or individuals. Indeed, such actions were critical to the actions against the apartheid era South African government and remain a significant point of contention, such as the

Table 1.2 A comparison of sanctions in the domestic and international context

	National sphere	*International sphere*
Meaning	Generally refers to a range of action that can be taken against a person who has transgressed a legal norm	The term 'sanctions' is commonly used to describe actions that often bear only a marginal resemblance to domestic sanctions.
Spectrum of action	A person who has committed a crime might receive the sanction of a prison term or prohibition of being able to engage in certain activities.	The spectrum of action commonly described as 'sanctions' includes military and non-military action.
Determination of the nature, scope of sanctions	National and regional legislatures	Individual states, groups of states, the international community as a whole, and non-state actors. National and regional legislatures with respect to the determination of the legislative basis for application.
Application	National judiciaries or juries	UN Security Council, UN General Assembly, International Court of Justice.
Enforcement	Police forces and penal systems	International Court of Justice; national courts.
Purposes	To enforce the law and to reinforce the rule of law, defining the limits of permissible behavior, punishing wrongdoers and deterring potential future wrongdoers.	To coerce the target into behaving in a particular manner, to negotiate regarding its behavior or to punish it for behavior considered unacceptable by the sender(s).

Source: After Farrall (2007) and Crawford (1999)

nonviolent Boycott, Divestment and Sanctions (BDS) movement for Palestinian rights (see also Chapter 3). However, it should be noted that in such cases the capacity to promote or operate is still going to be constrained by the legislation and policies of the sender country and, in some cases, by the potential for extra-territorial application of the domestic laws of the target state. In the case of the BDS movement there also appears to be sanctions against sanctions (Box 1.2).

Sanctions regimes usually contain a blend of different types of sanctions. These can be broadly divided into the categories of economic and financial sanctions and non-economic sanctions (Table 1.3). Economic sanctions

Box 1.1 Protest at sporting events – the 2019 Pan-Am Games

There has long been a tradition of protest at sport events. Perhaps most famously the black power/human rights salute used at the 1968 Mexico Olympics by African-American athletes Tommie Smith and John Carlos who raised a black gloved fist during the playing of the US anthem (the two athletes were subsequently banned from the Olympic Village and suffered substantial ostracism from the athletic community as a result of their actions). Together with Smith and Carlos Australia's Peter Norman, who finished second, all wore the Olympic Project for Human Rights (OPHR) badges. The aim of the OPHR was to protest against racial segregation in the US, Rhodesia, and South Africa and racism in sports in general and had promoted an unsuccessful boycott of the Mexico City Olympics as well as calling for the restoration of Muhammad Ali's world heavyweight boxing title and for Avery Brundage, who was accused of being an anti-Semite and Nazi sympathiser, to step down as President of the International Olympic Committee (Steen, 2012).

However, athletes who engage in human rights protests may be sanctioned by event organizers and/or international and national sporting bodies. Indeed, if public attendees to many international sporting events ever read the fine print of their ticket purchase there is usually a clause that states that they can be removed from the stadium or not allowed admittance if they are deemed to be engaging in overtly political activity. In August 2019 US gold medal winning fencer Race Imboden (also a Bronze medal Olympian) and gold medal winner hammer thrower Gwen Berry were threatened with sanctions by the United States Olympic and Paralympic Committee (USOPC). Part of the winning squad in the team foil event, Imboden dropped to one knee during the award ceremony as the US flag was raised in a political protest. The taking a knee protest was started in 2016 by then San Francisco 49ers quarterback Colin Kaepernick to highlight police shootings of unarmed black men. According to Imboden

> We must call for change . . . This week I am honored to represent Team USA at the Pan-Am Games, taking home gold and bronze. My pride however has been cut short by the multiple shortcomings of the country I hold so dear to my heart. Racism, gun control, mistreatment of immigrants, and a president who spreads hate are at the top of a long list. I chose to sacrifice my moment today at the top of the podium to call attention to issues

that I believe need to be addressed. I encourage others to please use your platforms for empowerment and change.

(quoted in Guardian sport and agencies, 2019)

Hammer thrower Gwen Berry raised her fist on the podium at the end of the national anthem after winning gold. According to Berry, 'I love representing my country. America is a great country. It's the best country in the world . . . However, what we are standing for right now, it is complete and utter – it's extreme injustice' (quoted in Guardian sport and agencies, 2019).

Both protests contravened an agreement US athletes signed that stated they will not 'make remarks or release propaganda of political, religious or racial nature, or any other kind' during the Pan Am Games. USOPC spokesman Mark Jones stated to Reuters

Every athlete competing at the 2019 Pan American Games commits to terms of eligibility, including to refrain from demonstrations that are political in nature . . . In this case, Race didn't adhere to the commitment he made to the organizing committee and the USOPC. We respect his rights to express his viewpoints, but we are disappointed that he chose not to honor his commitment. Our leadership are reviewing what consequences may result.

(quoted in Guardian sport and agencies, 2019)

Source: Guardian sport and agencies (2019)

Box 1.2 Omar Barghouti and the BDS movement

In April 2019 Omar Barghouti, a human rights defender and a co-founder of the Boycott, Divestment, Sanctions (BDS) movement for Palestinian rights was stopped and prevented from boarding his flight at Ben Gurion airport to attend a series of speaking engagements in the United States. The US consulate informed the airline staff that US immigration had banned him from entering the country, despite having a valid visa, without providing a reason and despite his previous regular visits there. According to Barghouti (2019) he has

been smeared by the Israeli government and banned from travel repeatedly, including in 2018 when I was prevented from going to Jordan to accompany my late mother during cancer surgery. Israel's intelligence minister threatened me with "targeted civil elimination", drawing condemnation from Amnesty International. Their de facto and "arbitrary travel ban" against me was recently lifted for three months after Amnesty International's pressure . . . Meanwhile, members of Congress and politicians in 27 states have passed laws intended to suppress the voices of Americans who support BDS. The ACLU has condemned these repressive measures as an unconstitutional violation of free speech that is "reminiscent of McCarthy-era loyalty oaths".

As Barghouti points out, opposition to the BDS campaign would appear to run against US traditions of free speech and the use of boycotts for social, political, and economic justice, including civil rights and discrimination on the basis of color, religion, and sexuality.

Source: Barghouti (2019)

Table 1.3 An overview of types of sanctions by sector or activity

Types of sanctions	Focus/purpose	Characteristics
Economic sanctions	Prevent the flow of commodities, products, and services to or from a target.	*Comprehensive sanctions*: describes a sanctions regime that seeks to prevent the flow to and from a target of all commodities, products, and services. *Particular sanctions*: prevent the flow to or from a target of specific commodities, products, and services.
Financial sanctions	Interrupt the ability of the target to engage in financial relations with the external world.	Freezing any financial resources or assets belonging to the target and prohibit the transfer of financial resources or assets, including insurance provision, to parties either located in the target or acting on behalf of parties located in the target.
Diplomatic and representative sanctions	Interrupt the official relations between a target and the external world to express disapproval through diplomatic and political means, rather than affect economic or military relations. Measures include limitations or cancellations of high-level government visits or expelling or withdrawing diplomatic missions or staff.	*Diplomatic sanctions* are applied against a target that is recognized as a state by the international community and therefore maintains diplomatic relations with other states. *Representative sanctions* are applied against a target that is not recognized as a state and whose official relations are more correctly described as 'representative' rather than 'diplomatic'.

Types of sanctions	Focus/purpose	Characteristics
Transport sanctions	Prevent or reduce transport connectivity, whether by land, sea, or air, to a target.	Closure or reduction in transport connections to or from the target with corresponding impacts on the mobility of people and products.
Travel sanctions (travel ban)	Prohibit or inhibit the ability of individuals associated with the target of a sanctions regime to travel internationally.	Travel sanctions may be applied against a target population, individuals and /or specific entities.
Aviation sanctions	Prohibit flights to and from a target or inhibit a target's ability to utilize flights within its own area of influence as well as affect international connectivity.	Ban all or reduce flights to and from a target; affect the operations of a target's national airline; prohibit the provision of technical assistance, advice, training, insurance, and insurance-related payments related to the use, manufacture or maintenance of aircraft within areas controlled by a target; and restrict use of target country's air space by third parties.
Sporting, cultural, intellectual, and scientific sanctions	Prohibit sporting, cultural, intellectual, and scientific relations between the target and the external world.	Prevent participation in sporting, scientific, and cultural events on the target's territory or that include official representatives of the target. Suspension of scientific and technical co-operation and cultural exchanges and visits involving persons or groups officially sponsored by or representing the target.
Telecommunication sanctions	Disrupt telecommunications between the target of a sanction's regime and the outside world.	Disrupt or restrict telephone or Internet connectivity of target state to outside world.

are usually the most important of all sanctions imposed on a country. They imply 'the deliberate, government-inspired withdrawal, or threat of withdrawal, of customary trade and financial relations' (Hufbauer et al., 1990, p. 2). As Crawford (1999, p. 5) well states

> the denial of customary interaction may take the form of embargoes of material and financial resources and products to the target, boycotts of target-state products, seizures of financial or real-estate assets held outside the target's borders, and isolation of the target in material economic

and social – diplomatic, cultural, and intellectual – realms. The target of sanctions may be simply the "state," but sanctions are better understood if targets are disaggregated.

An example of a state organizational sanction in the cultural realm is that of the China Film Administration boycott of the Golden Horse Awards, which take place in Taiwan, in 2019 (Box 1.3). Nevertheless, it is important to note that sanctions occur over different scales including multilaterally (at the UN or by a group of states with a common sanctions regime), regionally (the EU in particular but they may be conducted by any regional bloc), and unilaterally (e.g. US unilateral sanctions against different countries) (Happold & Eden, 2019). Sanctions can be also collective (universal), voluntary, or sometimes

---

Box 1.3 The Golden Horse Awards – the 'Chinese Oscars'

The Golden Horse Awards is one of the most prestigious events in the Chinese-speaking world, and in November, 2019 the awards were held in the capital of Taiwan, Taipei. Mainland Chinese actors and films have entered and won awards, in the past. However, in August 2019 China's film regulator, the China Film Administration, announced that it was banning mainland Chinese movies and stars from participating in the annual awards ceremony. No reason was given for the boycott, but it came after an escalation of tensions between China (People's Republic of China) and Taiwan (Republic of China) as a result of a proposed $2.2bn arms sale by the US to Taiwan and criticism of the USA for not adhering to a One China policy, under which the USA recognises and only has formal ties with mainland China. China had also stated that it would impose sanctions on US firms involved in the deal. China's foreign ministry spokesperson, Geng Shuang, said the US arms sale constituted 'a serious violation of international law and the basic norms governing international relations. . . . To safeguard our national interests, China will impose sanctions on the US enterprises involved in the above-mentioned arms sales to Taiwan' (Reuters in Beijing, 2019).

The previous year's ceremony also saw a number of participants air political views regarding the relationship between the two Chinas. In early August 2019 China also stated that it would stop issuing individual travel permits for Chinese visitors wanting to go to Taiwan because of the 'current cross-strait situation', something that would clearly impact Taiwan's tourism industry.

Source: BBC News (2019a)

citizen-initiated boycotts in the form of non-forceful coercive activities are also described as sanctions (Farrall, 2007). Table 1.4 summarizes different levels of sanction regimes while Figure 1.1 also illustrates some of the differences between smart/targeted and general boycotts and sanctions.

Table 1.4 An overview of types of sanctions by different scale of sanctions regime

Level of sanctions	*Meaning*	*Examples*
Unilateral	When one state initiates coercive action, its actions are commonly referred to as 'unilateral sanctions'.	US sanctions against Cuba, Iran, North Korea, Venezuela; Israeli sanctions (blockade) against the Gaza Strip.
Multilateral	When action is initiated by a group of states, the action becomes 'multilateral'.	UN sanctions against South Africa, Rhodesia, North Korea.
Regional	When action is initiated by a group of states at a regional organization level.	Sanctions against the former Yugoslavia by the European Union.
Collective/universal	When action is taken by a majority of states, it is referred to as 'collective' or 'universal' sanctions.	UN Sanctions.
Voluntary state sanctions	When other states are requested to take some voluntary and non-mandatory action against a sanctioned country.	In the cases of Southern Rhodesia and South Africa, prior to the eventual imposition of mandatory sanctions the Security Council requested states to take certain actions against Southern Rhodesia and South Africa, without requiring the application of such measures under Chapter VII. In the case of Cambodia, the Security Council requested states bordering Cambodia to prevent the import of timber products from Khmer-Rouge controlled areas.
Citizen-initiated boycotts	Non-forceful coercive activities initiated by non-state actors, such as citizen-initiated boycotts, are sometimes described as sanctions. Such campaigns can act as a domestic pressure on state foreign policy.	Campaigns against tourists visiting authoritarian states or those abusing or restricting human rights, such as campaigns against tourists visiting Myanmar or Brunei. The campaign against Brunei including calling for a boycott on hotel properties owned by the Sultan of Brunei.

Sources: Adapted from Wallensteen (2000), Hufbauer et al. (1990, 2008) and Farrall (2007)

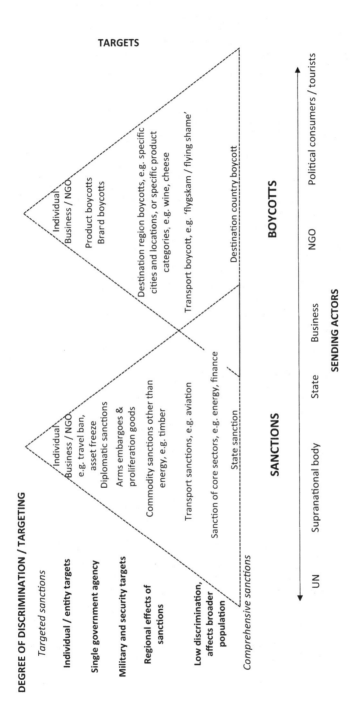

Figure 1.1 Degree of discrimination in sanction and boycott targeting by sending actors

Source: After Biersteker, Tourinho, and Eckert (2016), Seyfi and Hall (2019a, 2019b)

International sanctions in contemporary perspective

Multilateral level: UN Security Council

The United Nations Security Council has increasingly resorted to sanctions as part of its efforts to build peace and prevent conflict under the authority of Chapter VII of the United Nations Charter (Mack & Khan, 2000; Brzoska, 2003, 2015). Article 41 states

> The Security Council may decide what measures not involving the use of armed force are to be employed to give effect to its decisions, and it may call upon the Members of the United Nations to apply such measures. These may include complete or partial interruption of economic relations and of rail, sea, air, postal, telegraphic, radio, and other means of communication, and the severance of diplomatic relations (Charter of the United Nations, Chapter VII – Action with respect to Threats to the Peace, Breaches of the Peace, and Acts of Aggression, Article 41.

Sanction measures under Article 41 encompass a broad range of enforcement options that do not involve the use of armed force, and the majority of them have targeted state actors and have been imposed for a range of objectives, including compelling an occupying state to withdraw (e.g. Iraq's invasion of Kuwait); preventing a state from developing or acquiring weapons of mass destruction (e.g. North Korea, Iran, Iraq); countering international terrorism (e.g. Libya, Sudan, Taliban, Al Qaida, Hariri sanctions regimes); stemming human rights violations (e.g. Southern Rhodesia, South Africa, Haiti); and promoting the implementation of a peace process (e.g. Liberia, Rwanda, Sierra Leone, Ivory Coast) (Farrall, 2007). Security Council sanctions have taken a number of different forms in pursuit of a variety of goals. The measures have ranged from comprehensive economic and trade sanctions to more targeted measures such as arms embargoes, travel bans, and financial or commodity restrictions.

The first sanctions regime adopted by UN Security Council was in 1966 against the illegitimate seizure of power in Southern Rhodesia, while the most recent (as of July 2019) was regarding Mali, established on 5 September 2017, which was aimed at deterring spoilers of the peace process (Table 1.5). Since 2004, all new sanctions regimes have been targeted, comprising travel bans; assets freezes; arms embargoes; commodity bans (diamonds, timber, petroleum, charcoal); items, material, equipment, goods, and technology related to nuclear, ballistic missiles and other weapons of mass destruction programs, as well as bans on the export of certain luxury goods.

Table 1.5 The UN Security Council sanctions regime, 1966–2019

Resolution	Sanctions regime	Initiated	Terminated
232	Southern Rhodesia	1966	1979
418	South Africa	1977	1994
661	Iraq	1991	Continuing
713	Former Yugoslavia	1991	1996
733	Somalia	1992	Continuing
748	Libya	1992	2003
757	FRYSM (Federal Republic of Yugoslavia (Serbia and Montenegro))	1992	1996
788	Liberia	1992	2001
820	Bosnian Serbs	1993	1996
841	Haiti	1993	1994
864	Angola (UNITA) (National Union for the Total Independence of Angola)	1993	2002
918	Rwanda	1994	Continuing
1054	Sudan	1996	2001
1132	Sierra Leone	1997	Continuing
1160	FRY (the Federal Republic of Yugoslavia)	1998	2001
1267	Afghanistan/ Taliban/Al Qaida	1999	Continuing
1298	Eritrea and Ethiopia	2000	2001
1343	Liberia	2001	2003
1493	DRC (Democratic Republic of the Congo)	2003	Continuing
1521	Liberia	2003	Continuing
1556	Sudan	2004	Continuing
1572	Ivory Coast	2004	Continuing
1636	Hariri suspects	2005	Continuing
1718	North Korea	2006	Continuing
1737	Iran	2006	Continuing
1989	ISIL (Da'esh), Al-Qaida, Taliban and associated individuals and groups	2011	Continuing
1970	Libya	2011	Continuing
2084	Guinea-Bissau	2012	Continuing
2127	The Central African Republic	2013	Continuing
2140	Yemen	2014	Continuing
2206	South Sudan	2015	Continuing
2374	Mali	2017	Continuing

Identifying the target

As the Charter framework for collective security was designed to address disputes between states, the founders of the UN likely envisaged sanctions being applied against state targets. In practice, sanctions have been applied against a range of targets, including single and multiple states, failed states, as well as against pseudo-state, sub-state, and extra-state actors (Table 1.6). In addition, the practice of the Security Council demonstrates an increasing recognition of the desirability of applying measures that seek to impact decision-makers within the general group against which sanctions are imposed. When the Council imposes sanctions, it therefore undertakes a two-step process of targeting. The first step is to identify the general target against which the sanctions will be imposed, and the second step is to consider implementing measures that will directly target decision-makers within the general target.

Table 1.6 Different types of targets of UN sanctions

Targets	Explanation	Examples
Single state	Targeting single states and imposing sanctions against a functioning government and applying to the territory of the state as a whole.	South Africa, Iraq, Yugoslavia, Libya, Sudan, FRY, Liberia, North Korea, and Iran sanctions regimes.
Multiple state	Imposing sanctions against multiple state targets, in an attempt to resolve the conflict between them. In federal states, such as the former Yugoslavia, this involved action against multiple sub-states and emerging states.	Yugoslavia and Eritrea and Ethiopia.
De facto state	Denoting targets that are in de facto control of the machinery of government within a state but that are not recognized by the international community to be the legitimate – or de jure – government of that state.	Sanctions against illegal white minority regime led by Ian Smith in Southern Rhodesia; sanctions against the de facto government of Federal Republic of Yugoslavia (Serbia and Montenegro) (FRYSMO) led by Slobodan Milosevic), and sanctions against the Taliban regime in Afghanistan.
Failed state	Imposing sanctions against targets which effectively constitute failed states (i.e. in a state of chaotic civil war) with the aim of fostering peace and stability.	Somalia, Liberia, Rwanda, and Yemen.

(Continued)

Table 1.6 (Continued)

Targets	Explanation	Examples
Sub-state	The main characteristic of sub-state targets is that they operate within and tend to pose a threat to the peace and security of a state. In general, sub-state targets are rebel groups that seek to acquire control of the state from the existing government.	Bosnian Serbs, UNITA, rebel groups in Rwanda, rebel groups in Sierra Leone, and the Taliban. There may be overlap between sub-state and failed state targets.
Extra-state	An extra-state target is one which does not maintain a connection with a specific geographical base or operate solely within a particular state. This is a characteristic of international terrorist and criminal networks.	Usama Bin Laden and Al Qaida and their associates.
Individuals	Responding in part to a concern in respect to the unintended consequences of sanctions upon civilian populations, the Security Council has experimented with measures designed to ensure that its sanctions regimes have a more direct impact upon policy-makers and individuals whose actions have contributed to the relevant threat to international peace and security (e.g. by asset freezes and travel bans).	Travel restrictions and asset freezes against individuals in Iraq, North Korea, Iran, and individuals associated with Taliban and Al Qaida.

Source: After UN Security Council; Farrall (2007)

Regional level: EU sanctions

Restrictive measures or sanctions are an essential tool of the EU's Common Foreign and Security Policy (CFSP) (Koch, 2015; Kreutz, 2015; Portela, 2010, 2016). They are used by the EU as part of an integrated and comprehensive policy approach, involving political dialogue, complementary efforts, and the use of other instruments at its disposal (European Council, 2019). Table 1.7 provides an overview of sanctions adopted by the EU including those that fulfill UN sanctions regimes. Sanctions seek to bring about a change in the policy or conduct of those targeted, with a view to promoting the objectives of the CFSP. EU restrictive measures can be used to target:

- *governments* of non-EU countries because of their policies and actions;
- *entities* (companies or organizations) that provide the means to conduct the targeted policies and actions;
- *groups or organizations* such as terrorist or criminal groups; and
- *individuals* supporting the targeted policies, such as those involved in terrorist activities.

Table 1.7 EU sanctions: targets, type, and restrictive measures

Target	Specification (type)	UN	EU	Restrictive measures
Afghanistan	Restrictive measures imposed with respect to the Taliban	*		Arms export; freezing of funds and economic resources; restrictions on admission
Belarus	Restrictive measures against Belarus		*	Arms export; freezing of funds and economic resources; restrictions on admission; restrictions on equipment used for internal repression
Bosnia and Herzegovina	Restrictive measures in support of Bosnia and Herzegovina		*	Freezing of funds and economic resources; restrictions on admission
Burundi	Restrictive measures in view of the situation in Burundi		*	Freezing of funds and economic resources; prohibition to satisfy claims; restrictions on admission
Central African Republic	Restrictive measures against the Central African Republic		*	Arms export; freezing of funds and economic resources; restrictions on admission; prohibition to satisfy claims
China	Specific restrictive measures in relation to the events at the Tiananmen Square protests of 1989		*	Arms embargo
Democratic Republic of the Congo	Restrictive measures against the Democratic Republic of the Congo	*		Arms export; freezing of funds and economic resources; restrictions on admission; prohibition to satisfy claims
Egypt	Misappropriation of state funds of Egypt (MSF)		*	Freezing of funds and economic resources
Guinea (Republic of Conakry)	Restrictive measures against the Republic of Guinea		*	Freezing of funds and economic resources; restrictions on admission
Guinea-Bissau	Restrictive measures against those threatening the peace, security or stability of the Republic of Guinea-Bissau	*		Freezing of funds and economic resources; restrictions on admission

(Continued)

Table 1.7 (Continued)

Target	Specification (type)	UN	EU	Restrictive measures
Haiti	Prohibiting the satisfying of certain claims by the Haitian authorities		*	Prohibition to satisfy claims
Iran	Restrictive measures in relation to serious human rights violations in Iran (HR) and in relation to the non-proliferation of weapons of mass destruction (WMD)	*	*	Arms export; arms procurement; freezing of funds and economic resources; restrictions on admission; restrictions on equipment used for internal repression; telecommunications equipment; embargo on dual-use goods; inspections; restrictions on goods
Iraq	Restrictive measures on Iraq	*	*	Arms export; freezing of funds and economic resources; prohibition to satisfy claims; cultural property; petrol products
Lebanon	Restrictive measures in relation to the 14 February 2005 terrorist bombing in Beirut, Lebanon; restrictive measures in relation to the UN Security Council Resolution 1701 (2006) on Lebanon	*	*	Arms export; freezing of funds and economic resources; restrictions on admission
Libya	Restrictive measures in view of the situation in Libya and Prohibiting the satisfying of certain claims in relation to transactions that have been prohibited by the UN Security Council Resolution 883 (1993) and related resolutions	*	*	Arms export; arms procurement; freezing of funds and economic resources; flights, airports, aircrafts; inspections; ports and vessels; restrictions on admission; prohibition to satisfy claims; restrictions on equipment used for internal repression; vigilance
Maldives	Restrictive measures in view of the situation in the Republic of Maldives		*	Freezing of funds and economic resources; restrictions on admission
Mali	Restrictive measures in view of the situation in Mali	*	*	Freezing of funds and economic resources; restrictions on admission

Moldova	Restrictive measures in relation to the campaign against Latinscript schools in the Transnistrian region	*	Prohibition to satisfy claims
Montenegro	Prohibiting the satisfying of certain claims in relation to transactions that have been prohibited by the UN Security Council Resolution 757(1992) and related resolutions	*	Prohibition to satisfy claims
Myanmar (Burma)	Restrictive measures against Myanmar/ Burma	*	Arms export; freezing of funds and economic resources; dual-use goods export; restrictions on admission; restrictions on equipment used for internal repression; telecommunication equipment; restrictions on military training and military cooperation
North Korea	Restrictive measures in relation to the non-proliferation of the weapons of mass destruction (WMD)	*	Arms export; arms procurement; freezing of funds and economic resources; restrictions on admission; restrictions on goods; dual-goods export; financial measures; flights, airport and aircraft; inspections; investment; other restrictions: ports and vessels; aviation and jet fuel; crude oil; earth and stone; food and agricultural products; gold, precious metals, diamonds; luxury goods; machinery and electrical equipment; other items: petrol products; refined petroleum products; seafood; vessels; wood; industrial machinery, transportation vehicles, and iron, steel and other metals; restrictions on services; training and education; vigilance
Russia	Restrictive measures in view of Russia's actions destabilising the situation in Ukraine (sectoral restrictive measures)	*	Arms export and import; dual-use goods export; financial measures; prohibition to satisfy claims; restrictions on services; other items

(Continued)

Table 1.7 (Continued)

Target	Specification (type)	UN	EU	Restrictive measures
Serbia	Prohibiting the satisfying of certain claims in relation to transactions that have been prohibited by the UN Security Council Resolution 757(1992) and related resolutions		*	Prohibition to satisfy claims
Somalia	Restrictive measures against Somalia	*	*	Arms export; freezing of funds and economic resources; restrictions on admission; inspections; restrictions on admission; vigilance; other items
South Sudan	Restrictive measures in view of the situation in South Sudan	*	*	Arms export; freezing of funds and economic resources; restrictions on admission
Sudan	Restrictive measures in view of the situation in Sudan	*	*	Arms export; freezing of funds and economic resources; restrictions on admission
Syria	Restrictive measures against Syria and restrictive measures in relation to the 14 February 2005 terrorist bombing in Beirut, Lebanon	*	*	Freezing of funds and economic resources; restrictions on admission; arms export; financial measures; flights, airports, aircrafts; inspections; investments; prohibition to satisfy claims; restrictions on equipment used for internal repression; restrictions on goods; aviation and jet fuel; cultural property; gold, precious metals, diamonds; luxury goods; petrol products; telecommunications equipment; other items
Terrorism	Restrictive measures with respect to ISIL (Da'esh) and Al-Qaida (ISIL/Daesh & Al-Qaida)	*	*	Freezing of funds and economic resources; restrictions on admission; arms export; prohibition to satisfy claims
Tunisia	Misappropriation of state funds of Tunisia (MSF)		*	Asset freeze and prohibition to make funds available

Ukraine	Misappropriation of state funds of Ukraine (MSF); EU restrictive measures in respect of actions undermining or threatening the territorial integrity, sovereignty and independence of Ukraine (territorial integrity)	*	Freezing of funds and economic resources; restrictions on admission
	Restrictive measures in response to the illegal annexation of Crimea and Sevastopol (Crimea)	*	Financial measures; investments; restrictions on goods; restrictions on services
Venezuela	Restrictive measures in view of the situation in Venezuela	*	Arms export; freezing of funds and economic resources; restrictions on admission; restrictions on equipment used for internal repression; telecommunications equipment
Yemen	Restrictive measures in view of the situation in Yemen	*	Arms export; freezing of funds and economic resources; restrictions on admission; inspections
Zimbabwe	Restrictive measures against Zimbabwe	*	Arms export; freezing of funds and economic resources; restrictions on admission; restrictions on equipment used for internal repression

Source: Derived from Council of the European Union (2019)

Box 1.4 European Parliament recommends sanctions

In March 2019 the European Parliament approved a strongly worded resolution calling for sanctions and criticizing Nicaragua on its human rights record following a violent crackdown on protests demanding President Daniel Ortega leave office and allow early elections. The non-binding resolution on EU Policy asks the European Union's External Action Service and member nations for 'targeted and individual sanctions' such as visa bans and asset freezes against the Central American nation and 'individuals responsible for human rights abuses' until fundamental rights are restored and upheld. The measure was approved by a vote of 332 to 25, with 39 abstentions.

Source: Selser (2019)

Key objectives when adopting, sanctions are: safeguarding; EU's values, fundamental interests; and security preserving peace consolidating and supporting democracy, the rule of law, human rights; and the principles of international law preventing conflicts; and strengthening international security (European Council, 2019). Sanctions can also be imposed within the EU in order to address democratic deficits or 'backsliding' in its member states (Sedelmeier, 2017), although the EU has never used formal political sanctions against a member with Hellquist (2018) suggesting, 'whereas practical and symbolic distance-taking from the target is core for foreign policy sanctions, at home, the same ostracising properties run against the EU's traditional insistence on resolving disagreements through rational dialogue'. However, it should be noted that EU sanctions are put in place by the European Council and not the European Parliament, although the parliament may make recommendations that eventually lead to sanctions being put in place (Box 1.4).

Unilateral sanctions: the example of the US sanctions regime

Some US presidents use military force to impose America's will on other countries. Most prefer traditional diplomacy and negotiation, or else they ask allies to help them get their way. Jimmy Carter and Barack Obama stressed the importance of moral example in projecting global leadership. Donald Trump does things differently. Since taking office last year, he has repeatedly resorted to draconian economic sanctions and trade tariffs, launching them like missiles at countries and people he does not approve of. Trump did not invent the practice but it has become his foreign policy weapon of choice.

(Tisall, 2018)

The United States uses sanctions more than any other country (The Guardian, 2017). Economic sanctions have long been treated by American policymakers as a panacea for national security and other foreign policy challenges (Helms, 1999; O'Sullivan, 2010), and this can be seen in a wide range of sanctions imposed by different administrations as part of US foreign policy. This includes long running sanctions imposed against Cuba, North Korea, Iran, and Russia through to the most recent comprehensive sanctions against the Madero administration in Venezuela in response to the 2019 Venezuelan presidential crisis (Krauss, 2019). The scope of US sanctions is extensive and is illustrated in Table 1.8, which provides an overview of US broad-based and targeted sanctions as of 1 November 2018.

The USA's first major use of economic sanctions was the Jefferson trade embargoes (*Embargo Act of 1807*), in which the United States banned all exports to France and the United Kingdom in the hopes of pressuring them to cease their attacks on neutral American merchant ships during the Napoleonic wars (Sofka, 1997). From the Napoleonic period until entry into World War One the use of sanctions by the United States narrowed the scope of definitions of contraband and enlarged the rights of neutrals, although during the Civil War the North took a much broader interpretation against the South in seeking to win the war (Hufbauer, 1998). The passing of the *Trading With the Enemy Act* by Congress in 1917 gave the US President exceptionally broad powers to freeze foreign assets and regulate international finance and trade that continue to the present day (Hufbauer et al., 2008) and provide part of the legal basis for a number of US actions (see Table 1.8).

Sanctions have been used as a tool by different US administrations in an effort to dissuade nations from taking undesirable actions, e.g., supporting terrorism, proliferating weapons of mass destruction, violating human rights, trafficking in drugs, or despoiling the environment. However, in the climate of 9/11 and the subsequent US war against terrorism the US reshaped its foreign policy and its use of economic sanctions. Furthermore, the centrality of the US to the global financial system and the global power of the dollar provides a unique opportunity for US policymakers to strangle the target countries, entities, or groups through the banking sector via the extra-territorial reach of US legislation. Given the global financial system and hegemony of the US, all international banks cannot easily ignore access to the US financial system to function and clear US dollar transactions. This gives US financial sanctions an inherently long reach, ensuring that US

Table 1.8 US broad-based and targeted sanctions as of 1 November 2018

Sanctions	Focus of sanctions and controls	Domestic Legal Authority	UN Security Council Resolution
Balkans-Related	'the actions of persons engaged in, or assisting, sponsoring, or supporting, (i) extremist violence in the former Yugoslav Republic of Macedonia, in southern Serbia, the Federal Republic of Yugoslavia, and elsewhere in the Western Balkans region, or (ii) acts obstructing the implementation of the Dayton Accords in Bosnia or United Nations Security Council Resolution 1244 of 10 June 1999 in Kosovo, threaten the peace in or diminish the security and stability of those areas and the wider region, undermine the authority, efforts, and objectives of the United Nations, the North Atlantic Treaty Organization (NATO), and other international organizations and entities present in those areas and the wider region, and endanger the safety of persons participating in or providing support to the activities of those organizations and entities, including United States military forces and government officials' (Executive Order 13219).	Executive Orders: 13304 (29 May 2003), 13219 (27 June 2001) Statutes: *International Emergency Economic Powers Act; National Emergencies Act*	1244 (10 June 1999)

Belarus	'the actions and policies of certain members of the Government of Belarus and other persons to undermine Belarus' democratic processes or institutions, manifested most recently in the fundamentally undemocratic March 2006 elections, to commit human rights abuses related to political repression, including detentions and disappearances, and to engage in public corruption including by diverting or misusing Belarusian public assets or by misusing public authority' (Executive Order 13405).	Executive Order: 13405 (19 June 2006) Statutes: *International Emergency Economic Powers Act; National Emergencies Act*
Burundi	'the situation in Burundi, which has been marked by the killing of and violence against civilians, unrest, the incitement of imminent violence, and significant political repression, and which threatens the peace, security, and stability of Burundi' (Executive Order 13712).	Executive Order: 13712 (23 November 2015) Statutes: *International Emergency Economic Powers Act (IEEPA); National Emergencies Act*
Countering America's Adversaries Through Sanctions Act of 2017	Imposes new sanctions on Iran, Russia, and North Korea, including Iran's Islamic Revolutionary Guard Corps (IRGC).	Executive Order: 13848 (20 September 2014) Statutes: *Countering America's Adversaries Through Sanctions Act; Ukraine Freedom Support Act of 2014; Support for the Sovereignty, Integrity, Democracy, and Economic Stability of Ukraine Act of 2014*
Central African Republic	'the situation in and in relation to the Central African Republic, which has been marked by a breakdown of law and order, intersectarian tension, widespread violence and atrocities, and the pervasive, often forced recruitment and use of child soldiers, which threatens the peace, security, or stability of the Central African Republic and neighboring states' (Executive Order 13667).	Executive Order: 13667 (13 May 2014) Statutes: *International Emergency Economic Powers Act; National Emergencies Act*

(Continued)

Table 1.8 (Continued)

Sanctions	Focus of sanctions and controls	Domestic Legal Authority	UN Security Council Resolution
Counter Narcotics Trafficking	Deals with narcotics traffickers centered in Colombia and applies economic and other financial sanctions to significant foreign narcotics traffickers and their organizations worldwide	Executive Order: 12978 (22 October 1995) Statutes: *Comprehensive Addiction and Recovery Act of 2016; Foreign Narcotics Kingpin Designation Act; International Emergency Economic Powers Act; National Emergencies Act*	
Counter Terrorism	The sanctions cover a number of entities including the Palestinian Authority, Foreign Sanctions Evaders with Respect to Iran and Syria, Hizballah Bazzi Support Network, Haqqani Leaders, Taliban	Executive Orders: 13372 (16 February 2005); 13268 (2 July 2002); 13224 (24 September 2001); 13099 (21 August 1998); 12947 (23 January 1995). Statutes: *Hizballah International Financing Prevention Act of 2015; Antiterrorism and Effective Death Penalty Act of 1996; International Emergency Economic Powers Act; National Emergencies Act; United Nations Participation Act of 1945*	1526 (30 January 2004)

Program	Description	Authorities	UN Resolutions
Cuba	The most recent amendments were put in place on 9 November 2017. Under the amendments the Cuba embargo remains in place. Most transactions between the US – or persons subject to US jurisdiction – and Cuba continue to be prohibited. OFAC also issued changes to: restrict persons subject to US jurisdiction from engaging in direct financial transactions with entities and subentities identified on the State Department's List of Restricted Entities and Subentities Associated with Cuba ('Cuba Restricted List'), with certain exceptions; added requirements to certain categories of educational travel; removed the authorization for individual people-to-people educational travel; added requirements to the travel authorization *Support for the Cuban People*; and amended the definition of 'Prohibited officials of the Government of Cuba.'	Executive Order: 12854 (4 July 1993) Statutes: *Trade Sanctions Reform and Export Enhancement Act of 2000; Antiterrorism and Effective Death Penalty Act of 1996; Cuban Liberty and Democratic Solidarity (Libertad) Act of 1996; Cuban Democracy Act of 1992; Trading With the Enemy Act*	
Democratic Republic of the Congo-Related	Sanctions against persons contributing to the conflict in the Democratic Republic of the Congo	Executive Orders: 13671 (8 July 2014); 13413 (30 October 2006) Statutes: *International Emergency Economic Powers Act; National Emergencies Act; United Nations Participation Act of 1945*	1698 (31 July 2006); 1649 (21 December 2005); 1596 (18 April 2005)
Foreign Interference in a U.S. Election	Imposing certain sanctions in the event of foreign interference in a United States Election	Executive Order: 13848, (12 September 2018) Statutes: *International Emergency Economic Powers Act; National Emergencies Act*	
Global Magnitsky	The E.O. declares a national emergency with respect to serious human rights abuses and corruption globally, identifying these issues as threats to the national security, foreign policy, and economy of the United States.	Executive Order: 13818 (21 December 2017) Statutes: *Global Magnitsky Human Rights Accountability Act; International Emergency Economic Powers Act*	

(Continued)

Table 1.8 (Continued)

Sanctions	Focus of sanctions and controls	Domestic Legal Authority	UN Security Council Resolution
Iran	'4 November 2018 marked the final day of the 180-day wind-down period following the President's 8 May 2018 announcement to cease the United States' participation in the Joint Comprehensive Plan of Action (JCPOA). On 5 November 2018, the United States fully re-imposed the sanctions on Iran that had been lifted or waived under the JCPOA. These are the toughest U.S. sanctions ever imposed on Iran, and will target critical sectors of Iran's economy, such as the energy, shipping and shipbuilding, and financial sectors. The United States is engaged in a campaign of maximum financial pressure on the Iranian regime and intends to enforce aggressively these sanctions that have come back into effect . . . As part of the re-imposition of U.S. sanctions, in its largest ever single-day action targeting the Iranian regime, OFAC sanctioned more than 700 individuals, entities, aircraft, and vessels on 5 November 2018. This action was a critical part of the re-imposition of the remaining U.S. sanctions that were lifted or waived in connection with the JCPOA' (OFAC website).	Executive Orders: 13846 (6 August 2018); 13608 (1 May 2012); 13606 (23 April 2012); 13599 (6 February 2012); 13553 (29 September 2010); 13059 (20 August 1997); 12959 (7 May 1995); 12957 (16 March 1995); 12613 (29 October 1987); 12294 (26 February 1981); 12284 (23 January 1981); 12283 (23 January 1981); 12282 (23 January 1981); 12281 (23 January 1981); 12280 (23 January 1981); 12279 (23 January 1981); 12278 (23 January 1981); 12277 (23 January 1981); 12276 (January 2,3 1981); 12211 (17 April 1980); 12205 (17 April 1980); 12170 (14 November 1979) Statutes: Antiterrorism and Effective Death Penalty Act of 1996; Comprehensive Iran Sanctions, Accountability, and Divestment Act of 2010; Countering America's Adversaries Through Sanctions Act; Iran Freedom and Counter-Proliferation Act of 2012; International Emergency Economic Powers Act; Iran Sanctions Act of 1996; International Security and Development Cooperation Act of 1985; Iran Threat Reduction and Syria Human Rights Act of 2012; National Defense Authorization Act for Fiscal Year 2012; National Emergencies Act; Trade Sanctions Reform and Export Enhancement Act of 2000.	2231 (20 July, 2015); The provisions of Security Council resolutions 1696 (2006), 1737 (2006), 1747 (2007), 1803 (2008), 1835 (2008), 1929 (2010), with respect to the Nuclear Non-proliferation Treaty and 2224 (2015) were terminated subject to re-imposition in the event of significant non-performance of JCPOA commitments.

Iraq-Related	'In response to Iraq's invasion of Kuwait on 2 August 1990, the United States imposed comprehensive sanctions, including a trade embargo against Iraq and a freeze of the assets of the then-Iraqi government . . . Over the years, a series of Executive orders adjusted the sanctions in response to events in Iraq. . . . There currently are no broad-based sanctions in place against Iraq, but there are certain prohibitions and asset freezes against specific individuals and entities associated with the former Saddam Hussein regime, as well as parties determined to have committed, or to pose a significant risk of committing, an act of violence that has the purpose or effect of threatening the peace or stability of Iraq or the Government of Iraq or undermining efforts to promote economic reconstruction and political reform in Iraq or to provide humanitarian assistance to the Iraqi people' (OFAC Overview of Sanctions).	Executive Orders: 13668 (27 May 2014); 13438 (17 July 2007); 13364 (29 November 2004); 13350 (30 July 2004); 13315 (29 August 2003); 13303 (22 May 2003); 13290 (20 March 2003); 12817 (23 October 1992); 12724 (9 August 1990); 12722 (2 August 1990) Statutes: *Antiterrorism and Effective Death Penalty Act of 1996; International Emergency Economic Powers Act; National Emergencies Act; United Nations Participation Act of 1945* 1483 (22 May 2003); 1293 (31 March 2000); 1284 (17 December 1999); 1175 (19 June 1998); 1158 (25 March 1998); 1153 (20 February 1998); 1143 (4 December 1997); 1129 (12 September 1997); 1111 (4 June 1997); 1051 (27 March 1996); 986 (14 April 1995); 778 (2 October 1992); 706 (15 August 1991); 687 (8 April 1991); 670 (25 September 1990); 661 (6 August 1990)
Lebanon-Related	OFAC has implemented a Lebanon sanctions program since 1 August 2007, when the President issued Executive Order 13441, *Blocking Property of Persons Undermining the Sovereignty of Lebanon or Its Democratic Processes and Institutions.*	Executive Order: 13441 (1 August 2007) Statutes: *International Emergency Economic Powers Act; National Emergencies Act*

(Continued)

Table 1.8 (Continued)

Sanctions	Focus of sanctions and controls	Domestic Legal Authority	UN Security Council Resolution
Libya	'the ongoing violence in Libya, including attacks by armed groups against Libyan state facilities, foreign missions in Libya, and critical infrastructure, as well as human rights abuses, violations of the arms embargo imposed by United Nations Security Council Resolution 1970 (2011), and misappropriation of Libya's natural resources threaten the peace, security, stability, sovereignty, democratic transition, and territorial integrity of Libya' (Executive Order 13726).	Executive Orders: 13726 (19 April 2016); 13566 (25 February 2011) Statutes: *International Emergency Economic Powers Act; National Emergencies Act*	
Magnitsky	The Act provides authority for the identification of and imposition of sanctions on certain persons related to the detention, abuse, and death of Sergei Magnitsky or responsible for certain gross violations of human rights in the Russian Federation.	Statutes: *Sergei Magnitsky Rule of Law Accountability Act of 2012; International Emergency Economic Powers Act*	
Non-Proliferation	Designed to combat the proliferation of weapons of mass destruction (WMD) and the means of delivering them. Initially applied to eight organizations in North Korea, Iran, and Syria but has also been used with respect to the conversion of highly enriched uranium extracted from Russian nuclear weapons into low-enriched uranium for use in commercial nuclear reactors.	Executive Orders: 13608 (1 May 2012); 13382 (29 June 2005); 13094 (29 July 1998); 12938 (14 November 1994) Statutes: *International Emergency Economic Powers Act; National Emergencies Act*	1929 (9 June 2010); 1803 (3 March 2008); 1747 (24 March 2007); 1737 (23 December 2006); 1696 (31 July 2006); 1540 (28 April 2004)

North Korea	Blocks the Government of North Korea and the Workers' Party of Korea; prohibits the exportation and reexportation of goods, services (including financial services), and technology to North Korea; and prohibits new investment in North Korea	Executive Orders: 13810 (21 September 2017); 13722 (16 March 2016); 13687 (2 January 2015); 13570 (18 April 2011); 13551 (30 August 2010); 13466 (26 June 2008) Statutes: *Antiterrorism and Effective Death Penalty Act of 1996; Countering America's Adversaries Through Sanctions Act; International Emergency Economic Powers Act; National Emergencies Act (NEA); North Korea Sanctions and Policy Enhancement Act of 2016; United Nations Participation Act of 1945*	2397 (22 December 2017); 2375 (11 September 2017); 2371 (5 August 2017); 2356 (2 June 2017); 2321 (30 November 2016); 2270 (2 March 2016); 2094 (7 March 2013); 2087 (22 January 2013); 1874 (12 June 2009); 1718 (14 October 2006)
Rough Diamond Trade Controls	'In the Interlaken Declaration of 5 November 2002, representatives of the United States and 47 other countries announced the launch of the Kimberley Process Certification Scheme for rough diamonds ("KPCS"). Countries participating in the KPCS ("Participants") are expected to prohibit the importation of rough diamonds from, and the exportation of rough diamonds to, non-Participants and to require that shipments of rough diamonds from or to a Participant be controlled through the KPCS' (OFAC Overview of Sanctions).	Executive Order: (30 July 2003) Statutes: *Clean Diamond Trade Act; International Emergency Economic Powers Act (IEEPA); National Emergencies Act (NEA); Section 5, United Nations Participation Act of 1945*	

(Continued)

Table 1.8 (Continued)

Sanctions	Focus of sanctions and controls	Domestic Legal Authority	UN Security Council Resolution
Somalia	'The United Nations Security Council has played an active role in relation to Somalia since establishing an arms embargo in 1992 following the collapse of the Somali regime. Since 2001, the Council has issued 17 United Nations Security Council Resolutions (UNSCRs), concerning the continued instability, tension, and violence in the country, as well as the reoccurring acts of piracy and armed robbery at sea off the coast of Somalia". OFAC has implemented a sanctions program relating to Somalia since 2010 "to deal with the national emergency posed by the escalation of violence in Somalia by targeting persons engaging in acts threatening the peace, security, or stability of Somalia, including the terrorist organization al-Shabaab' (OFAC Overview of Sanctions).	Executive Orders: 13620 (20 July 2012); 13536 (13 April 2010) Statutes: *International Emergency Economic Powers Act; National Emergencies Act; United Nations Participation Act of 1945*	1897 (30 November 2009); 1872 (26 May 2009); 1851 (16 December 2008); 1846 (2 December 2008); 1844 (20 November 2008); 1816 (2 June 2008); 1772 (20 August 2007); 1744 (20 February 2007); 1725 (6 December 2006); 1356 (19 June 2001); 733 (23 January 1992)
Sudan and Darfur	An OFAC license is required for certain exports and reexports to Sudan of agricultural commodities, medicine, and medical devices as a result of Sudan's inclusion on the State Sponsors of Terrorism List (SST List). Specific sanctions exist related to the conflict in Darfur.	Executive Orders: 13804 (11 July 2017); 13761 (13 January 2017); 13412 (13 October 2006); 13400 (27 April 2006); 13067 (4 November 1997) Statutes: *Darfur Peace and Accountability Act of 2006; Trade Sanctions Reform and Export Enhancement Act of 2000; Antiterrorism and Effective Death Penalty Act of 1996; International Emergency Economic Powers Act; National Emergencies Act; United Nations Participation Act of 1945*	1672 (25 April 2006); 1591 (29 March 2005)

South Sudan-related	Deals with the situation in and in relation to South Sudan, which has been marked by widespread violence and atrocities, human rights abuses, recruitment and use of child soldiers, attacks on peacekeepers, and obstruction of humanitarian operations	Executive Order: 13664 (3 April 2014) Statutes: *International Emergency Economic Powers Act; National Emergencies Act*	
Syria	Deals with the Government of Syria's policies in supporting terrorism, continuing its occupation of Lebanon, pursuing weapons of mass destruction and missile programs, and undermining US and international efforts to stabilize Iraq. Following events in Syria beginning March 2011, subsequent orders were issued in response to the ongoing violence and human rights abuses taking place in Syria. The Syria sanctions program is one of the most comprehensive US sanctions programs.	Executive Orders: 13608 (1 May 2012); 13606 (23 April 2012); 13582 (18 August 2011); 13573 (18 May 2011); 13572 (29 April 2011); 13460 (15 February 2008); 13399 (26 April 2006); 13338 (12 May 2004) Statutes: *Antiterrorism and Effective Death Penalty Act of 1996; International Emergency Economic Powers Act; Iran Threat Reduction and Syria Human Rights Act of 2012; International Emergency Economic Powers Act; National Emergencies Act*	1636 (31 October 2005); 1595 (7 April 2005)
Transnational Criminal Organizations	Deals with 'the growing threat of significant transnational criminal organizations. The President found that the activities of significant transnational criminal organizations had reached such scope and gravity that they threaten the stability of international political and economic systems . . .such organizations were becoming increasingly sophisticated and dangerous to the United States, because they were increasingly entrenched in the operations of foreign governments and the international financial system, thereby weakening democratic institutions, degrading the rule of law, and undermining economic markets' (OFAC Overview of Sanctions).	Executive Orders: 13581 (25 July 2011) Statutes: *International Emergency Economic Powers Act; National Emergencies Act*	

(Continued)

Table 1.8 (Continued)

Sanctions	Focus of sanctions and controls	Domestic Legal Authority	UN Security Council Resolution
Ukraine-/ Russia-related	Deals with the threat posed by the actions and policies of certain persons who had undermined democratic processes and institutions in Ukraine; threatened the peace, security, stability, sovereignty, and territorial integrity of Ukraine; and contributed to the misappropriation of Ukraine's assets. In further response to the actions and polices of the Government of the Russian Federation, including the purported annexation of the Crimea region of Ukraine (OFAC Overview of Sanctions).	Executive Orders: 13849 (20 September 2018); 13685 (19 December 2014); 13662 (20 March 2014); 13661 (17 March 2014); 13660 (6 March 2014) Statutes: *Countering America's Adversaries Through Sanctions Act*; *Ukraine Freedom Support Act of 2014*; *Support for the Sovereignty, Integrity, Democracy, and Economic Stability of Ukraine Act of 2014*; *International Emergency Economic Powers Act*; *National Emergencies Act*	
Venezuela-related	'in light of actions by the Maduro regime and associated persons to plunder Venezuela's wealth for their own corrupt purposes, degrade Venezuela's infrastructure and natural environment through economic mismanagement and confiscatory mining and industrial practices, and catalyze a regional migration crisis by neglecting the basic needs of the Venezuelan people' (Executive Order, 1 November 2018).	Executive Orders: *Blocking Property of Additional Persons Contributing to the Situation in Venezuela* (1 November 2018); 13835 (21 May 2018); 13827 (19 March 2018); 13808 (24 August 2017); 13692 (8 March 2015) Statutes: *Venezuela Defense of Human Rights and Civil Society Act of 2014*; *International Emergency Economic Powers Act*; *National Emergencies Act*	

Yemen-related	Deals with 'the actions of individuals and entities that directly or indirectly threaten the peace, security, or stability of Yemen, including obstructing the implementation of the 23 November 2011 Gulf Cooperation Council (GCC) initiative between the Government of Yemen and those in opposition to it' (OFAC Overview of Sanctions).	Executive Order: 13611 (16 May 2012) Statutes: *International Emergency Economic Powers Act; National Emergencies Act* 2216 (14 April 2015); 2204 (24 February 2015); 2201 (15 February 2015); 2140 (26 February 2014)
Zimbabwe	Deals with 'specifically identified individuals and entities in Zimbabwe, as a result of the actions and policies of certain members of the Government of Zimbabwe and other persons undermining democratic institutions or processes in Zimbabwe' (OFAC Overview of Sanctions).	Executive Orders: 13469 (25 July 2008); 13391 (23 November 2005); 13288 (7 March 2003) Statutes: *International Emergency Economic Powers Act; National Emergencies Act*

Source: Derived from OFAC (2019)

designations can make a bank toxic on the international scene (Bey, 2018). Different US administrations have had different approaches towards sanctions, either to be unilateral or multilateral. Bey (2018) explains that:

> In moving against the United States' foes, Presidents George W. Bush and Barack Obama were content to largely act in a multilateral fashion, usually under the auspices of the U.N. Security Council. But President Donald Trump who has taken the same tools crafted under the previous two administrations and supercharged them has made it abundantly clear that he is willing to go it alone in pursuing America's enemies. And given Trump's unilateral approach when it comes to pressuring China, the World Trade Organization and others on trade, as well as his distaste for multilateral institutions, it is not inconceivable that his administration will eventually push for unilateral sanctions on someone other than Iran.

In 2017 the US Treasury imposed sanctions on 944 foreign entities and individuals – a record (Tisdall, 2018). This number has since been supplanted. The Trump administration's reliance on economic sanctions as a foreign policy tool and the Office of Foreign Assets Control's continued emphasis on pursuing sanctions against violators has created vast challenges for multinational and regional companies, while the evolving enforcement landscape has expanded the risk of enforcement action and reputational damage that may occur as a result (Box 1.5). The increased use of sanctions is set to continue giving rise to new risks and opportunities for businesses and entities. Furthermore, it raises a critical question, does the use of sanctions and tariffs as a foreign policy tool actually work? Tisdall's response to this is salutary

> The White House claims its "maximum pressure" campaign against North Korea succeeded in bringing Kim Jong-un to the negotiating table in June. But while the summit strengthened the North Korean dictator, Trump's main aim – denuclearisation of the Korean peninsula – remains as elusive as ever. In this case and others, critics say, sanctions are a substitute for thought-through policy.
>
> Trump's sanctions on Iran are likewise in danger of backfiring politically. The measures have principally succeeded in uniting warring hardline and moderate leadership factions in shared defiance of Washington. More significantly, in terms of Middle East peace, Iran may retaliate by forcibly halting all regional oil exports via the Gulf and the Red Sea if the US embargo goes ahead. The result of Trump's bully-boy tactics could be a global oil shock – and military confrontation in the Strait of Hormuz.
>
> (Tisdall, 2018)

Box 1.5 Standard Chartered fined by the US for sanctions breaches

In April 2019 the British bank Standard Chartered agreed to pay $947m to American agencies, including the US Department of Justice, over allegations of 'apparent violations' of US sanctions imposed against Burma, Cuba, Iran, Sudan, Syria, and Zimbabwe. The US Department of Treasury said that the processed transactions were worth $438m between 2009 and 2014, the majority of which involved Iran-linked accounts from its Dubai branch routing payments through, or to, its New York office or other banks based in the US. In 2012 Standard Chartered had paid $667m to settle US allegations of sanctions breaches between 2001 and 2007. According to US Assistant Attorney General, Brian Benczkowski: 'Today's resolution sends a clear message to financial institutions and their employees: if you circumvent US sanctions against rogue states like Iran – or assist those who do – you will pay a steep price' (quoted in Makortoff, 2019). The bank will remain in deferred prosecution agreement (DPA) with the US Department of Justice and the New York county district attorney's office, which allows firms to settle charges with state authorities without facing criminal prosecution, until April 2021.

Source: Makortoff (2019)

Effectiveness of sanctions

The widespread use of economic and other sanctions constitutes one of the great paradoxes of contemporary foreign policy even though they are becoming the policy tool of choice for many international bodies and countries in the post-Cold War world (Weiss, 1999; Hufbauer et al., 2008; Brzoska, 2015). The defense of sanctions adoption in general, as a foreign policy instrument, was premised on the expectation that sanctions would offer an alternative to the use of force (Carneiro & Apolinário, 2016). Nevertheless, despite the widespread use of sanctions and the extensive range and number of sanctions regimes by different international actors applied at different scales, e.g. countries, sectors, products, firms, and individuals, there is a growing debate as to their effectiveness in enacting policy change in the target country (Pape, 1997; Galtung, 1967; Hufbauer et al., 2008; Brzoska, 2015). Smeets (2019) observes that: 'The number of sanction episodes seems to be on the rise and sanctions have increasingly gained in popularity in recent years and such

---

Box 1.6 US sanctions on Venezuela and human rights

In August 2019 the UN High Commissioner for Human Rights, Michelle Bachelet, criticized an extension of US sanctions targeting the Venezuelan government and the economic activities of its authorities, because of their potential to exacerbate suffering among the wider population. Although the US sanctions include exceptions for transactions with Venezuelan authorities related to certain food, clothing, and medicine, in a statement Bachelet said

> I am deeply worried about the potentially severe impact on the human rights of the people of Venezuela of the new set of unilateral sanctions imposed by the US this week. . . . The sanctions are extremely broad and fail to contain sufficient measures to mitigate their impact on the most vulnerable sectors of the population. However, they are still likely to significantly exacerbate the crisis for millions of ordinary Venezuelans.

Source: AFP in Geneva (2019)

---

despite the fact that the literature does not present conclusive evidence that economic sanctions are an effective policy instrument'.

Moreover, several analyses document the unanticipated adverse consequences that economic sanctions have in the target country and they have identified adverse consequences in the realm of human rights protection, economic development, the prospects for democracy, and other political dynamics (Cortright & Lopez, 2000, 2002; Carneiro & Apolinário, 2016). According to a 2013 comprehensive study, UN targeted sanctions have been assessed to be effective in coercing a behavioral change in 10% of cases (Biersteker, Eckert, Tourinho, & Hudáková, 2013). They are more successful in constraining negative behavior (in 28% of cases) and in signalling support for international normative frameworks (in 27% of cases). While intended as a nonviolent foreign policy alternative to military intervention, sanctions have often worsened humanitarian and human rights conditions in the target country (Wood, 2008) although sanctions are often specifically imposed on the premise of improving human rights (Peksen, 2009) (see Box 1.6).

Peksen (2009) analyzed the effects of sanctions on human rights in countries targeted with economic sanctions and offers an empirical examination of the effects of sanctions on the physical integrity rights of citizens in target countries for the period 1981–2000. He concludes that economic sanctions worsen government respect for physical integrity rights, including freedom from disappearances, extra-judicial killings, torture, and political imprisonment. He also suggests that multilateral sanctions have a greater overall negative impact on human rights than unilateral sanctions. In a similar study, Wood (2008) examines the relationship between economic sanctions and state-sponsored repression of human rights. Drawing on both the public choice and institutional constraints literature, he argues that the imposition of economic sanctions negatively impacts human rights conditions in the target state by encouraging incumbents to increase repression. He further explains that sanctions threaten the stability of target incumbents, leading them to augment their level of repression in an effort to stabilize the regime, protect core supporters, minimize the threat posed by potential challengers, and suppress popular dissent. In giving the example of sanctions regime against Iraq in 1990s, Bey (2018) argues that:

> Sanctions destroyed the country's economy and the health of the nation's citizens in the process yet failed to achieve their desired political goal: force Saddam Hussein to alter his behavior. If anything, Saddam's personal wealth and power even increased during the period. What's more, the measures engendered a popular resentment against the United States that continues in some parts of the country to this day.

According to Hall (2005), sanctions are viewed as a type of 'carrot-and-stick' diplomacy in dealing with international trade and politics and are also criticized for being too effective due to the devastating impact they can have on innocent civilian populations. Sanctions have been described as 'the UN's weapon of mass destruction' (Halliday, 1999; Mueller & Mueller, 1999), as 'a genocidal tool' (Simons, 1999; Bisharat, 2001), as 'modern siege warfare' (Gordon, 1999), and as 'economic terrorism' (Axelrod, 2018). Surprisingly, various countries subjected to sanctions (e.g. Iran, Cuba, North Korea, or Zimbabwe) have proven to be extremely resilient to the long-standing economic and foreign policy pressures levelled against them (Grauvogel & von Soest, 2013). Such a situation reflects the complexity of sanctions as a foreign policy tool but also highlights the importance of understanding their impacts.

Summary and conclusions

This chapter began with a piece from a Guardian editorial from 2017 that was discussing the merit of President Trump's signing into law new sanctions against Russia. The sub-heading for the editorial stated that, 'Neither pure diplomacy nor outright war, sanctions are often better than both' (The Guardian, 2017). However, while this may be the case it is notable that the editorial urged great caution in their use. Although noting that smart sanctions 'are more desirable than blanket ones that risk coming across as collective punishment, or can be diverted by autocrats to feed their regime's cronyism and corruption' the editorial went on to stress, 'Left in place for too long sanctions can also become a hindrance, if not an embarrassment. . . . Coercion – coordinated by groups of nations – can be legitimately used to uphold international norms, such as human rights conventions, but is much less legitimate when it serves one country's interests alone' (The Guardian, 2017). Indeed, it is interesting to note that rather than preventing conflict, the first recorded sanctions undertaken by Pericles against Megara 'ultimately helped to trigger the Peloponnesian War. One can only hope that in this century, wiser heads will prevail, and that economic sanctions lead to bargaining, not violence' (Rogoff, 2015).

This first chapter has sought to briefly outline the nature and scope of sanctions. To some readers the sheer scale of UN, EU, and US sanctions may come as a surprise. However, it also highlights the extent to which sanctions can directly and indirectly affect many different destinations and businesses, their competitors, and the patterns and flow of international travellers. As the chapter stresses, despite concerns over their effectiveness, sanctions have grown in use. Their use, along with other measures such as changes in tariffs and manipulation of exchange rates, have become an integral component of economic statecraft. Nevertheless, sanctions go beyond the economic and can also be applied to cultural, educational, and sporting interactions. All of these areas are of interest to the student of tourism as is the contribution that sanctions make to consumer perceptions of potential destinations and the long-term relations between the sender of sanctions and the target.

The historical context of sanctions shows that while remaining a constant foreign policy element for the past 200 years their focus has changed over time. Yet they are now more important than ever given the growing number of sanctions that are being enacted. It is not yet clear whether we are moving into a new period of sanction use marked by even more aggressive use of targeted and so-called smart sanctions or whether they have become a component of economic warfare. Regardless, sanctions are an integral component of seeking to understand the emerging geopolitics of tourism in the 21st century, an issue that the next chapter examines in close detail.

2 Sanctions and tourism

Introduction

As the opening chapter highlighted, sanctions are increasingly being used by major actors in the international political system, such as the United Nations Security Council, as instruments to address major challenges to international peace and security (UN Security Council, 2019) as well as further national and collective interests. In foreign policy terms sanctions are seen as an essential tool by the EU as part of an integrated and comprehensive policy approach to safeguarding the EU's values, fundamental interests, and security, preserving peace and preventing conflicts and strengthening international security (European Commission, 2019) and by the world's major powers to promote their foreign policy agendas (Lopez & Cortright, 2018; Dalton, 2019). As Chapter 1 highlighted the United States is foremost among countries in using economic statecraft, including sanctions, to achieve diplomatic and foreign policy goals.

There exists a wide body of academic literature concerned with what motivates countries to impose sanctions in the first place and whether and under what conditions sanctions succeed in achieving the objectives of those countries that impose them, as well as to assessing how sanctions affect political economy in those countries that are targeted by sanctions (Connolly, 2018). Although it has also been argued that the impacts of sanctions do not necessarily follow, that impact leads to effectiveness. A target country that suffers a reduction in the availability of goods or capital or which experiences a reduction in GDP or number of international tourists as a direct result of sanctions may be said to have been impacted by sanctions. But the target government may not be prompted to modify the policy or action that caused sanctions to be imposed in the first place (Connolly, 2018).

The practice of sanctions is among the most widely-explored in international relations and political sciences (e.g. Kunz, 1960; Nossal, 1989; Pape, 1997; Drezner & Drezner, 1999; Hufbauer et al., 2008; Taylor, 2012; Servettaz, 2014; Lopez & Cortright, 2018; Jaeger, 2018; Dalton, 2019).

Sanctions have also been explored in other fields including economics (e.g. Porter, 1979; Dajani & Daoudi, 1983; Leogrande, 1996; Gurvich & Prilepskiy, 2016; Korhonen, Simola, & Solanko, 2018; Drezner, 2015); political economy (e.g. Frank, 2006; Kaempfer, & Lowenberg, 2007; Eyler, 2007; Fischhendler, Herman, & Maoz, 2017); international law (Kunz, 1960; Reisman & Stevick, 1998; Joyner, 2018); geopolitics (Wood, 2007); public policy (Alexander, 2009); and political geography (Bassett & Hoare, 1987; Bhungalia, 2010; Christopher, 1994; Mercille, 2008) among others. Nevertheless, despite its significance for travel flows and the tourism industry, there is surprisingly little research on sanctions in a tourism context despite their substantial impact on and relationship to tourism (Seyfi & Hall, 2019a, 2019b). The studies that have been undertaken from a tourism context have tended to focus on particular cases of sanctions and the associated impacts and response. Table 2.1 provides an outline of some of the cases where tourism has been affected by sanctions and the associated literature.

As Table 2.1 indicates the sanctions literature in tourism has tended to focus on the sanctions operating on developing countries although this does not negate the particular economic importance that tourism may have for the sanctioned countries, e.g. Cuba, South Africa, and Zimbabwe. It is only since 2015 that countries that are, or were, major tourism destinations (Turkey) or a major tourism generating area (Russia) in absolute terms, have become subject to sanctions. The Russian Federation, an important tourism

Table 2.1 Indicative examples of sanctions literature in tourism

Sanctions case	Indicative examples
Cuba	Macaulay (2007), Kendrick, Fullerton, & Broyles (2015), Wilson and Látková (2016), and Gordon (2016)
Myanmar	Philp and Mercer (1999), Henderson (2003), and Reith and Nauright (2005)
North Korea	Connell (2017) and Xizhen and Brown (2000)
Iran	Khodadadi (2016a, 2016b), Pratt and Alizadeh (2018), Seyfi, Hall, and Kuhzady (2019), and Seyfi and Hall (2019a, 2018b, 2018c, 2018d)
Palestine	Isaac, Hall, and Higgins-Desbiolles (2015)
Syria	Moret (2015)
South Africa	Pirie (1990)
Rhodesia/Zimbabwe	Galtung (1967)
Russia	Ovcharov, Ismagilova, Ziganshin, and Rysayeva (2015), Ivanov, Sypchenko, and Webster (2017), and Dreyer and Popescu (2014)
Turkey	Cetin, Akmese, Aras, and Aytekin (2016), and Şahin, Konak, and Karaca (2017)

generating market and destination, received sanctions following its annexation of Crimea, and Turkey was affected by Russian sanctions on travel to Turkey, following the shooting down of a Russian military aircraft in 2015 (see Box 2.1). However, such work has tended to be relatively descriptive

---

Box 2.1   Russian sanctions against Turkey

In retaliation for the shooting down of a Russian warplane by Turkish fighters on the Syria-Turkey border in November 2015, Russia swiftly imposed a raft of economic sanctions and punitive measures against Turkey that considerably affected Turkish businesses in general, e.g. construction firms and food exports and tourism industry in particular. There were also restrictions on Turkish companies operating in Russia and Turkish citizens working for companies registered in Russia, and Russia suspended work on TurkStream pipeline project (an alternative to Russia's South Stream pipeline to transport gas to Europe without crossing Ukraine). The latter was important as Turkey relies on Russia for 55% of its annual natural gas needs. Furthermore, there was also some suggestion that non-listed export goods (e.g. textiles) were subject to an unofficial ban on imported Turkish goods by the Russian government. Overall estimates indicate that the wide range of sanctions cost Turkey at least $10bn (£7bn) in lost business.

The Turkish tourism industry was profoundly and immediately affected by sanctions that banned charter flights between the two countries, which substantially affected Russian tour operators selling trips to Turkey and modified the visa regime between the countries. Natali Tours, one of Russia's biggest tour operators, suspended sales of packages to Turkey (Novoderezhkin, 2015). Pegas Touristik, one of the largest Russian travel agencies, canceled all its bookings for Turkey until 2016. On 27 January 2016, following the threats of the Islamic State, Rostourism, the federal tourism agency, warned Russians on holiday in Turkey against the risk of kidnapping by Daesh terrorists (Harrus, 2015).

The sanctions and restrictions against Turkey substantially affected Russians arrivals in Turkey. Until this event Russia had been the second most imported tourist generating country to Turkey after Germany. Turkey's seaside Mediterranean resorts, e.g. Antalya, were among the popular holiday destinations for Russians given their geographical closeness, the holiday facilities designed in accordance with the preferences of Russian visitors, visa facilities, and the long tourism season in terms of climate. In 2015, a total of 5.6 million Russian tourists spent their holidays in Turkey. In December 2015, the number of Russian tourists in Turkey fell by 46% compared to December 2014. For the period from January to April 2016, the percentage of Russian visitors dropped between 68% to 79.3% on a monthly basis. The number of Russian tourists coming to Antalya for the same period declined by 90.5% (Cetin et al., 2016). As a consequence, many tourism and hospitality businesses were hugely impacted, and it was estimated that Turkey lost $3.5bn in annual income from Russian tourists. Taking advantage of this situation, countries such as Italy, Israel, and Bulgaria increased their promotions to attract Russian tourists. Although the countries that benefited most were Greece, Cyprus, and Bulgaria, where the Schengen visa is easier to obtain than the Crimea; countries of the former USSR such as Kyrgyzstan; and Tunisia (Harrus, 2015). Russia did not relax the trade sanctions placed on Turkey until June 2017.

Source: Girit (2016)

with sanctions usually being framed as an economically focused geopolitical tool while the multi-scaled socio-cultural and environmental dimensions of sanction have largely been overlooked. In addition, much of the current literature does not explains how tourism in countries exposed to sanctions and boycotts are affected and continue to operate, with perhaps notable exceptions being the cases of Palestine (Isaac et al., 2015) and Iran (Seyfi & Hall, 2018a). A further comment on the tourism and sanctions literature is that much of it is comparatively recent. This is perhaps a reflection of two things. First, international tourism only really expanded from the late 1960s on as a result of the advent of jet aircraft and the jumbo jet in particular. Second, tourism-specialist journals and tourism-focused researchers did not emerge to any degree until the late 1970s, with tourism studies often not being portrayed as a serious subject by other social science disciplines, thereby also delaying research in the area.

This chapter seeks to identify how sanctions affect tourism and hospitality industry at a number of levels, ranging from the international to the individual and the implications of such actions for tourism policy, marketing, and destinations. In addition, the chapter will identify some of the coping responses of sanctioned destinations including the difficulties that arise in destination management and marketing in a sanctioned country. The chapter commences with a brief discussion of geopolitics, sanctions, and tourism before examining some of the ways that tourism is affected by sanctions: mobility constraints, diplomatic sanction, and flight bans.

Geopolitics, sanctions, and tourism

Sanctions are a popular tool of foreign policy and a tactic that involves sanctioning actors to achieve their strategic goals by persuading or punishing other governments or political actors to change their policies and behavior. Nevertheless, the evolution of competing interests and strategic priorities, rather than the economic pressure of sanctions, mainly informs and shapes the trajectory of strategic objectives and the decision taken by policy makers. Sanctions and economic pressure are merely tactics states use to pursue their goals, and as realities change governments often opt to shift tactics (Bayer, 2016). This can be witnessed in a range of sanctions imposed that show that the sanctions regimes differ significantly in design, scope, and ultimately impact. For example, sanctions imposed on Russia by the US and its allies, mainly European Union countries, in 2014 were designed to pressure Moscow by creating long-term costs for Russia (e.g. targeting individuals, targeting energy and defense companies and financial institutions by restricting foreign investment and their access to western credit markets and their freezing of asset) without sacrificing the West's ability to cooperate with Russia on other issues (e.g. Syria crisis). In contrast, Iran's sanctions particularly those constructed in 2012 were designed to cripple the country's economy in the short term and bring Tehran to the negotiating table over its nuclear program, e.g. European Union ban on oil imports from Iran and US efforts to isolate Iran from the international financial system. The sanctions had a significant negative impact on Iran's economy. However, it was ultimately the regional balance of power and shifting realities on the ground (instability in Iraq and the rise of the Islamic State that led to convergence of strategic interests for Iran and US and EU), rather than financial pressures, that led to the nuclear deal between Iran and world powers in 2015 and a partial lifting of sanctions. By comparing the sanctions regime on Russia and Iran Bayer (2016) explains that:

> Sanctions on Russia were designed to demonstrate that the West disapproves of the annexation of Crimea and fighting in eastern Ukraine without fully alienating the Russian regime, thus allowing for continued cooperation on issues ranging from arms control to Syria. In Iran, the sanctions regime was designed to isolate the country and push the regime into a corner. But as Western and Iranian geopolitical goals began converging, both Iran and Western governments became more

amenable to concessions. In both cases, however, evolving interests, rather than economic pressure, play a dominant role in shaping the trajectory of negotiations and the use of sanctions as a tool.

Tourism has become a focus – or casualty of foreign policy decision-making although its importance is usually underestimated in international politics (Hall, 2005). Nevertheless, the relationship between tourism and geopolitics in the academic literature has generally been characterized by mutual neglect. Weaver (2010, p. 48) explains that:

> Contemporary geopolitical discourses rarely mention tourism, and the tourism literature is rarely, if ever, framed within an explicitly geopolitical context. This is despite the fact that international tourism is an inherently geopolitical phenomenon involving the mass movement of people across international boundaries, made possible only through the exercise of the sovereign powers of both the origin and destination state.

The growth of interest in geopolitics in tourism studies (e.g. Hall, 2017; Weaver, 2010) highlights the ways in which international tourism is an implicitly geopolitical activity, e.g. working relationships between blocs, countries, international organisations, and regions; growing international mobility; cross-border flows of capital, commodities, and workforce; and a range of specific international agreements that cover tourism flows, development, and investment (Hall, 1994a; Hall, & O'Sullivan, 1996; Reiser, 2003; Coles & Hall, 2008; Hannam, Butler, & Paris, 2014; Webster & Ivanov, 2017).

Geopolitical theorising has gradually come to acknowledge that geopolitical contestation needs to move beyond the realm of the nation-state and be more broadly framed as an area for sub-state and private actors, as well as the mobility of individuals within geopolitical systems (Hall, 2017). As Dalby (2013, p. 18) observes, 'It is about the spaces of politics, the geographies of rule, authority and frequently violence. It is nearly always about attempts to make, organize, dominate and control particular spaces' including the spaces of the neoliberal economy.

The combination of multiple scales and actors and acknowledging the mobility of human subjects, as well as resources and communication, has led to greater recognition that tourism is also subject to the outcomes of geopolitical activity (Hall, 2017). The spatial consequences of international relations is evidenced at supranational and national levels along with activity at subnational levels – both at destinations and at international borders – and local tourism-related responses to such impacts and reterritorialisation in the form of the increased relevance of location and characteristics of place (Hazbun, 2004).

Tourism's relationship to sanctions therefore engages with conventional geopolitical theory, which is focused on the role of the nation state and spatial political governance, as well as the more recent developments with respect to critical geopolitics, which encompass a more diverse range of academic challenges to the conventional ways in which political space is written, read, and practiced (Power & Campbell, 2010; Hall, 2017). The latter is engaged in the 'analysis of a range of enduring global challenges like environmental catastrophe, new modes of war, persistent global inequalities, imperial desires and reductive representations' (Power & Campbell, 2010, p. 245), including in the context of tourism (Saldanha, 2002; Attanapola & Lund, 2013; Ho, 2013). Interest in the role of sanctions is therefore not just about their use as foreign policy instruments – as important as that is – but also with respect to the economic and behavioral responses to sanctions and their connection to the wider socio-economic system and the different levels of the tourism system. As such, research on sanctions provides a potential new direction in critical geopolitical studies given its capacity to highlight the effects of the denial or constraint of movement as well as the way in which tourism is bound up in resistance to sanctions (Seyfi & Hall, 2019a, 2019b).

Sanctions and mobility

Freedom of movement, mobility rights, or the right to travel is a human rights concept encompassing the right of individuals to travel from place to place within the territory of a country and to leave the country and return to it (Gilbert, 2014). Such a right is provided in the constitutions of numerous states and in documents reflecting norms of international law. For example, Article 13 of the Universal Declaration of Human Rights (UDHR) asserts that:

> a citizen of a state in which that citizen is present has the liberty to travel, reside in, and/or work in any part of the state where one pleases within the limits of respect for the liberty and rights of others, and that a citizen also has the right to leave any country, including his or her own, and to return to his or her country at any time.

Nowadays given the advances, more and more people have the economic means and opportunities to travel freely compared to the past, and yet, the freedom of movement and the right to travel are far from being globally recognized as human rights (Torabian & Miller, 2017) and are often overshadowed by issues of race, gender, ethnicity, nationality, religion, sexuality, and politics. Indeed, while international travel is often associated with notions of freedom the reality is that there is no automatic right to travel in international law. While Caruana and Crane (2011, p. 1495) point out, 'tourism is inexorably tied up in notions of freedom' their work suggests three main notions of freedom within contemporary tourism: as an individual motivation; as a tourism narrative; and as an outcome of relationships between tourism stakeholders. To this we can also add the political freedom to travel. However, there is no international right to travel to another country. Even the often cited UDHR is advisory and, as seen earlier, only postulates a right of exit and entry to one's own country and freedom of mobility within it. Instead rights to travel need to be understood via the framework of international governance and law and, in specific cases, from national and supranational law. Citizens have legal rights to travel in some countries and, hence, depart, but they may not have rights to enter their proposed destination, i.e. are not able to obtain a visa. Citizenship does not automatically entitle rights of exit or access. As Coles (2008, p. 67) observed of EU Accession in 2004 and of the potential expansion of the Schengen Zone, 'it is all well and good to be offered the right to travel but this is meaningless if the right to entry is restricted'. Indeed, with an original list of 73 countries, the number of countries facing common visa restrictions to all Schengen countries increased to 108 in the 1995 regulation and to 132 in the 2001 regulation (Neumayer, 2006; Hall, 2013).

The significance of legal restrictions to entry is substantial as they provide a basis for the implementation of sanctions on cross-border mobility. However, the legal dimension of international mobility is inseparable from the political and social dimensions, meaning that legislative and regulatory sanctions on movement can also mean that potential visitors encounter discriminatory actions in the form of xenophobia, racism, and more recently, Islamophobia (Torabian & Miller, 2017). Increasing regulation and heightened security for travel to and within some countries can affect international travel flows (Hall, 2005) and tourists' travel decisions and experiences. Furthermore, the discourses of racialized identities in travel and tourism have implications in terms of denial of entry and admission to a nation state and tightened border crossings and national securities and contesting individuals' rights to travel.

Tourism and international movement as proposed within the rights highlighted by UN rights and global discourses is meant to be a freedom ideally attainable and practiced by all individuals. Yet, as noted above, these mobility rights are restricted in a number of ways by various governments. One notable example is the executive order signed by United States President Trump on 27 January 2017, temporarily suspending entry of individuals from seven countries (i.e. Iran, Iraq, Libya, Somalia, Sudan, Syria, and Yemen) and placing restrictions on visa renewals for an additional 38 countries. However, the Trump measures do not represent a new development in the US use of restricting mobility. For example, there are longstanding US restrictions on its citizens traveling to Cuba as part of a US strategy to encourage the Cuban state communist government to reform its politics and economy and also to stop its support of other countries in the region, such as Venezuela (see Box 2.2). In addition to these blanket restrictions

---

Box 2.2 Cuba's tourism in the face of long-running US embargo against Cuba

The United States began an embargo against Cuba on 19 October 1960 when the latter nationalized US-owned oil refineries on Cuban soil and without compensation. At first the embargo prohibited all exports from the US to Cuba except for medicine and food but was later expanded to cover almost all exports. It is the longest trade embargo in modern history (Gordon, 2016).

The US–Cuba relationship has been plagued by distrust and antagonism since 1959, the year Fidel Castro overthrew a US-backed regime in Havana and established a socialist state allied with the Soviet Union. During the half century that followed, successive US administrations pursued policies intended to isolate the island country economically and diplomatically.

Tourism industry in Cuba was substantially affected due to the travel ban to Cuba by United States citizens, which is one of the most long-standing bans on travel and mobility to a destination. Under President Barack Obama, the US eased several restrictions with Cuba, permitting, among other things, educational tours, commercial air travel, and cruises of the island for American citizens. The US also reopened its embassy in Havana, and Cuba reopened its embassy in Washington (Wilson & Látková, 2016). However, more recently, the US announced major new restrictions on US citizens traveling to Cuba blocking the most common way Americans are able to visit the island through organized tour groups that license US citizens to travel automatically and banning US cruise ships from stopping in the country (Oppmann & Vazquez, 2019). American tourism is not explicitly permitted in Cuba. However, Americans could travel to Cuba if it was covered under specific categories, which included organized group travel, known as group people-to-people travel. However, the Trump administration banned travel to the island taken in this category as well despite those trips having been undertaken by thousands of American citizens. Yet, travel for university groups, academic research, journalism, and professional meetings is continuing to be allowed as of late 2019 (Oppmann & Vazquez, 2019).

on mobilities that are associated with power and government (Bærenholdt, 2013), there are also travel bans, in the form of blacklisting and the restrictions on admission, imposed as a part of smart sanctions on individuals and entities in target countries.

Targeted sanctions

The international relations landscape has witnessed a qualitative shift from economic sanctions against states, popular in the post-Cold War era, towards the smart and targeted sanctions that are deployed with increasing scope and effect in the post-9/11 era (Cameron, 2003, p. 227). De Goede (2011) explains that:

> Targeted sanctions arose out of a political critique of more traditional UN Security Council sanctioning regimes as directed at states. In particular, the economic sanctions against Iraq in the 1990s led to a profound critique of the ways in which sanctions affect a corrupt regime's civilian population through restrictions on imports of food and consumer goods.
>
> (2011, p. 501)

Thus, this reform in sanctions policy provided a basis for sanctioning actors to use targeted sanctions as a viable alternative to target power elites and ruling classes than states as a whole or innocent population (Cortright & Lopez, 2018b). This has been seen in the cases of UN sanctions against Taliban, ISIL, and other terrorist groups. As is explained in Resolution 1373 (2001), adopted in the wake of 9/11, all states shall:

> Freeze without delay funds and other financial assets or economic resources of persons who commit, or attempt to commit, terrorist acts or participate in or facilitate the commission of terrorist acts; of entities owned or controlled directly or indirectly by such persons; and of persons and entities acting on behalf of, or at the direction of such persons and entities, including funds derived or generated from property owned or controlled directly or indirectly by such persons and associated persons and entities.
>
> (United Nations Security Council, 2001, p. 2)

Travel bans and visa restrictions against individuals not only avoid the possible humanitarian impacts of broader travel restrictions but also are believed to be useful in denying legitimacy to political leaders, military officials, and their supporters. A notable example is the European Union 'blacklist' of Serbian President Milosevic's supporters. The 600 individuals on the blacklist are prohibited from traveling in Europe and their assets in European banks are frozen. Hufbauer and Oegg (2000) argue that:

> While Milosevic and his supporters benefited from the Serbian trade embargo by controlling the profitable black market, they do seem to mind personal international isolation. They find themselves hobbled in conducting business abroad: the travel ban cuts them off from their companies and bank accounts.

Blacklisting of specific named individuals or organizations in the form of asset freeze and travel ban is one of the most popular tactics in the smart and targeted sanctions. The rationale behind such measures is on the basis of suspicion that they are involved in the financing or facilitation of terrorism (De Goede, 2011). There are now an estimated 214 blacklists in operation worldwide, of which the UN Security Council 1267 Sanctions List, the US Office of Foreign Asset Control (OFAC) list and the EU financial sanctions list are undeniably the most important (see Box 2.3).

Box 2.3 OFAC Specially Designated Nationals and Blocked Persons List (SDN)

The Specially Designated Nationals list (SDN) is a group of organizations and individuals who are restricted from doing business with the United States, American companies, or general Americans. This includes terrorist organizations, individual terrorists, and state sponsors of terrorism. The list of specially designated nationals is maintained by the U.S. Department of The Treasury Office of Foreign Assets Control (OFAC). Collectively, such individuals and companies are called 'Specially Designated Nationals' (SDNs). Their assets are blocked, and US persons are generally prohibited from dealing with them. The OFAC SDN list represents a tool in the fight against money laundering and terrorist financing in the United States and around the world. It forms part of the US Treasury's Selective Sanctions policy in which specific individuals and organizations involved in certain criminal activities are penalized, as opposed to the more comprehensive approach of sanctioning entire nations. As of 2019 OFAC's Specially Designated Nationals and Blocked Persons List ("SDN List") has approximately 6,300 names connected with sanctions targets. OFAC also maintains other sanctions lists, which have different associated prohibitions.

The Specially Designated Nationals and Blocked Persons List is updated regularly with the names of individuals, entities, and organizations deemed to be involved in a range of criminal activities. US Persons (US citizens and permanent resident aliens regardless of location, US incorporated entities and their foreign branches, and in some circumstances their subsidiaries) are prohibited from doing business with anyone on the OFAC SDN list – and need to check the list to ensure they are not in breach of the law if there is any uncertainty. Businesses should also conduct checks prior to establishing a relationship with a foreign person or entity or conducting transactions with them and periodically throughout the relationship if there is potential for them to be on the list.

See: www.treasury.gov/about/organizational-structure/offices/Pages/Office-of-Foreign-Assets-Control.aspx

Yet the effectiveness of travel bans as a tool has been criticized for its limited results. By taking the example of the travel and flight ban imposed on Libya in response to the bombing of Pan Am 103, Hufbauer and Oegg (2000) argue that:

> In the case of Libya, one needs to remember that Qaddafi handed over the Pan Am 103 suspects to an international court only after the UN travel ban was falling apart. The ban was crumbling because the Organization of African Unity called on its members and others to suspend compliance with the ban. This sequence suggests that the travel ban at most had a minor impact on Qaddafi's decision to comply with the UN Security Council demands.

Diplomatic sanctions

Diplomatic sanctions are political measures taken to express disapproval or displeasure at a certain action through diplomatic and political means, rather than affecting economic or military relations. Measures include limitations or cancellations of high-level government visits or expelling or withdrawing diplomatic missions or staff. Table 2.2 summarizes some of the different forms of diplomatic sanctions. Diplomatic sanctions or sanctions characterized by political disengagement are seen as a low-cost means of isolating and delegitimizing regimes (Maller, 2010). Diplomatic sanctions also need to be understood within the wider context of the different international relationships that a state has. For example, the signing of the peace treaty

Table 2.2 Examples of different forms of diplomatic sanctions

Types of diplomatic sanctions	*Examples*
Closure of an embassy	US after Iran's revolution of 1979
	Closure of Saudi Arabia's embassy in Iran following attack on its embassy in Tehran
Temporary or lengthy cessation of formal diplomatic contact (Recall an ambassador for consultations)	The United States recalled its ambassador to Syria for consultations in 2005 following the assassination of Prime Minister Rafik Hariri of Lebanon
Withholding recognition of a particular regime or state for a period of time	The United States withheld recognition of many of the former Soviet republics when they originally announced their independence
Limiting number of diplomats allowed to work in the country/limit diplomatic presence	Strategy often applied between the United States and the Soviet Union/Russian Federation
Visa ban for certain political figures and officials	Applied by the Trump presidency against select Iranian figures and officials. Applied by Israel against US members of the House of Representatives
Embassy and all of the sending countries' property is placed under the custody of a protecting power	Switzerland takes on protecting power mandate for Iran and Saudi Arabia following attack on the Saudi embassy in Tehran in 2016
Downgrading diplomatic representation/relations (from ambassador to a chargé d'affaires)	In 1990 the United States cut off economic aid and military assistance to Myanmar and downgraded diplomatic relations

between Egypt and Israel in Washington, DC, in March 1979, following the 1978 Camp David Accords, is usually portrayed in the West as being a diplomatic success (Quandt, 2016). However, the treaty came at a huge political, diplomatic, and economic cost to Egypt in the Arab and Muslim world, with the country being suspended from several international organizations, severed international relations with many Arab countries in the region, and a substantial impact on the tourism economy (Box 2.4).

Diplomatic sanctions, however, entail a number of often overlooked consequences for the sanctioning' country. There have been two different approaches to this. One approach emphasized the need for greater engagement with problem states through diplomacy and the proponents of this approach argue that diplomacy is necessary, even with these regimes. Critics, however, maintain that engagement with these regimes is tantamount to appeasement and signals acceptance of behavior that ought to be condemned.

Box 2.4 The economic embargo of Egypt by Arab states in 1979

The Egypt – Israel Peace Treaty was signed in Washington, DC, on 26 March 1979, following the 1978 Camp David Accords, by Egyptian president Anwar Sadat and Israeli Prime Minister Menachem Begin and witnessed by United States president Jimmy Carter. This treaty was received with enormous controversy across the Arab world, and in response to it Arab countries imposed extensive political and economic sanctions against Egypt. Many Arab countries broke off their diplomatic ties with Egypt, and Egypt was suspended from the Arab League from 1979 to 1989. In addition, many financial and technical organizations, including the Arab Monetary Fund, the Islamic Conference, and the Organization of Arab Petroleum Exporting Countries (OAPEC) also suspended Egypt's membership.

Anger was such that Egyptian President Sadat was assassinated on 6 October 1981 by members of the Egyptian Islamic Jihad. This political controversy happened in a climate where throughout much of the 1970s economic ties between Egypt and the rest of the Arab world had become much more extensive. Egypt received substantial aid from Arab countries, especially after the 1973 war with Israel. Tourism from Arab states was increasing, accounting for more than 50 per cent of visitors prior to sanctions. The number of Egyptian workers in neighboring oil countries had also grown, as had their remittances back to Egypt, and trade in goods and services between Egypt and other Middle Eastern countries was expanding. Nevertheless, although the peace treaty had a positive impact on Egyptian-Israeli bilateral relations, it received huge criticism among Arab countries and had a major impact on the relationship between Egypt and its neighboring Arab countries despite their economic and political linkages (Lavy, 1984).

In the light of the Arab sanctions against Egypt, tourist flows to the country were immediately and substantially affected. This was significant as Egypt was a popular tourism destination among the countries in the Arab League. The tourism industry, while contributing only 2.3% to the GNP in 1971, was a major earner of foreign exchange, accounting for 14 per cent of the total exports. By 1976 income from the sector had reached 5.3% of GNP and 21 per cent of total exports, with tourism with Arab countries being the most important contribution. Arab tourism had grown throughout most of the 1970s to account for over 800,000 people by 1976. In 1977 the number of Arab tourists declined by 12% or 60,000 people. This downward trend continued through 1978 and became even more pronounced in 1979, with Arab tourism reaching its lowest level in some years (397,000 visitors). International tourism from Arab countries was extremely important as it served to compensate for the number of Western tourists visiting Egypt who were very sensitive to the political situation in the region, which fell drastically during and immediately after the Egyptian-Israeli wars of 1956, 1967, and 1973 (Lavy, 1984).

Interestingly in light of trying to understand the broader implications of economic and diplomatic sanctions on tourism, the Baghdad summit, which coordinated the Arab world's response to the Egyptian-Israeli Peace Treaty, did not specifically impose sanctions against tourism. Nevertheless, the media coverage in Arab countries together with the generally negative atmosphere created by the sanctions reduced the willingness of Arab tourists to visit Egypt with growth back to 1976 levels not occurring until 1981.

In their view, there is little to be gained by talking to these states, and they emphasize cutting diplomatic ties with these countries. Maller (2010, p. 61) criticizes the second view and argues that:

The potential costs of diplomatic sanctions include not only a substantial loss of information and intelligence on the target state, but also a reduction in communication capacity and a diminished ability to influence the target state. Ironically, diplomatic sanctions may even undermine the effectiveness of other coercive policy tools, such as economic sanctions. These adverse effects ought to cause policymakers to reassess the value of diplomatic isolation as a tool of foreign policy and recognize the inherent value of diplomatic engagement.

Although studies of sanctions tend to focus primarily on economic sanctions, diplomatic sanctions have been used repeatedly by the major powers (e.g. United States) against problematic states. The United States has employed them in conjunction with approximately 30% of its economic sanction episodes (O'Sullivan, 2010). Diplomatic sanctions can take a variety of forms, differing in both severity and duration. Modern-day diplomatic sanctions have primarily been used to target states for issues related to terrorism, proliferation, and an accompanying desire for regime change in some cases (Maller, 2010). For instance, following the invasion of Kuwait by Iraq in the early 1990s, the US severed its diplomatic ties with Iraq, and it only reestablished its diplomatic presence after Saddam Hussein was deposed following the 2003 invasion of Iraq. Similarly, in 1990 the United States cut off economic aid and military assistance to Myanmar and downgraded diplomatic relations along with a number of other Western nations (Hall, 1994b). A somewhat unusual sanction was Israel's announcement in 2019 that they would not allow entry to two US members of the House of Representatives on a Congressional trip, a decision that was publicly encouraged by the US President (Box 2.5). From a tourism perspective diplomatic sanctions are important because they can substantially affect the capacity to travel between countries either because of difficulties in accessing diplomatic and consular representatives or because of delays in visa processing. In addition, diplomatic sanctions can also affect perceptions of safety and security.

Box 2.5 Barring representatives Ilhan Omar and Rashida Tlaib from entering Israel

One of the most remarkable diplomatic/political sanctions in recent times was the announcement in August 2019 that Israel planned to bar members of the US House of Representatives Ilhan Omar and Rashida Tlaib from entering the country for a planned congressional trip to the West Bank and Jerusalem due to their support of the Boycott, Divestment and Sanctions (BDS) movement. Israel's parliament, the Knesset, passed a law in 2017 allowing the government to not grant visas or deport people who support a boycott of Israel or Jewish settlements in the occupied West Bank. Israel had previously denied entry or visas to other supporters of the boycott, but it was extremely unusual to do so to US politicians. What made it all the more amazing was that the Netanyahu's administration announced that Omar and Tlaib would be barred from entry only minutes after President Trump had tweeted 'It would show great weakness if Israel allowed Representative Omar and Representative Tlaib to visit. They hate Israel & all Jewish people, & there is nothing that can be said or done to change their minds' (quoted in Goldberg, 2019) thereby, suggesting that a US President was seeking to actively encourage a foreign power to sanction elected US Representatives from making a congressional trip to that country. Representative Tlaib was subsequently granted permission to visit her grandmother in the West Bank 'on the condition that she pledges not to act to promote boycotts against Israel', although this was subsequently rejected (Holmes, 2019).

Flight ban

Aviation bans fall into restrictions on all air travel to and from a target country or areas under control of targeted groups, with the premise being that the flight ban will substantially affect people in power while exerting minimal humanitarian impact on the general population (Hufbauer & Oegg, 2000). However, this assumption has been subject to debate. For example, in the case of a flight ban imposed on Sudan in 1996 by the UN Security Council for its suspected support of international terrorism, the implementation of the ban was delayed and eventually never implemented as the report of the UN Department of Humanitarian Affairs indicated that the ban would affect humanitarian aid and cause suffering in the wider population. This was because the Sudanese airline relied on international airports for aircraft maintenance, and a ban would have created severe problems for relief organizations that rely on the airline to reach remote areas of the country.

Another example is the case of the self-styled Turkish Republic of Northern Cyprus, which has been under substantial embargoes since its unilateral declaration of independence in 1983. The International Civil Aviation Organization and the International Air Transport Association are among the institutions that refuse to deal with the Turkish Cypriot community. As a result, flights to and from Northern Cyprus take place through Turkey, with direct international flights from elsewhere being banned together with direct flights by major airlines.

In 2019 Germany banned Iran's second-largest flight carrier, Mahan Airlines from operating in the country's airports after the EU had placed sanctions on Iran (Williams, 2019). This was because of ongoing suspicions of Iranian terrorist activities in Europe and accusations that this airline is used for military purposes and spying. Mahan Air was also blacklisted by the US in 2011, as Washington said the carrier was providing technical and material support to an elite unit of Iran's Revolutionary Guards known as the Quds Force. The US treasury has also threatened sanctions against countries and companies offering the airline's 31 aircraft landing rights or services such as on-board dining (Williams, 2019). The EU sanctions also reflected the US pressure on European countries to reimpose sanctions on Iran after President Donald Trump pulled Washington out of a nuclear non-proliferation treaty it had reached with Tehran under his predecessor Barack Obama.

Another example of flight bans being imposed was by Russia in response to anti-Russian protests and unrest in Tbilisi, Georgia. Georgia is usually one of the top destinations for Russian tourists, thanks to its Black Sea resorts, with 1.3 million visiting in the summer of 2018. The bans meant that Russia stopped all passenger flights to and from Georgia for an initially unspecified period of time. Travel companies were advised by the Russian government to stop selling holiday packages to Georgia, while Russian tourists already in the country were told to return home. It was estimated that the flight ban could cost Georgia as much as $300m, which amounts to almost 10% of Georgia's $3.2 billion tourism revenue in 2018 and that the six Russian airlines operating flights to the nation could lose $47.7m in refunds (The Moscow Times, 2019). It was not the first time Putin's government had suspended flights to Georgia with air travel between the two nations being cut in October 2006 and again in August 2008.

The impacts of sanctions on tourism

Although sanctions are an important tool in diplomacy, foreign policy, and global governance, sanctions regimes can have serious impact on the overall level of a targeted country's economic development and productivity, including the tourism industry, which is directly and indirectly affected by sanctions (Hall, 1994a). As shown in Figure 2.1, sanctions can be broadly categorized into four main types including financial, sectoral, diplomatic, and individual sanctions. Each of these sanctions has different implications for tourists and the tourism industry. The impacts of sanctions on tourism can also be understood as occurring in three inter-related areas: the macroeconomic environment, direct impacts, and indirect impacts (primarily societal impacts). At the macro level, both the supply and demand side of the economy are affected by sanctions. Sanctions usually have a negative impact on economic growth and result in significant inflationary pressures. Sanctions also tend to have a damaging effect on the purchasing power of people in the target country as a result of exchange rate impacts and reduced supply of imported products leading to price increases unless regulated. For example, Iranians' living standards were adversely affected as a result of sanctions, with Iranian workers losing an estimated 90% of their purchasing power over the sanctions period (Seyfi & Hall, 2018a, 2018b). Sanctions can also negatively influence the socio-economic status of the population in sanctioned countries by increasing levels of poverty and widening income disparities between rich and poor. For example, in 2016 it was estimated that over 25% of Iranians were living below the absolute poverty line and 30% under the relative poverty line (Seyfi & Hall, 2018a).

Given their scope sanctions clearly have direct economic impacts on the tourism industry. Generally, sanctions directly affect tourism arrivals, which then leads to a decline in tourism receipts and increased unemployment (Pratt & Alizadeh, 2018). Although the rationale behind broad sanctions as a foreign policy element is often to encourage people in sanctioned countries to actively influence their government they often fail to do so and are often regarded by the majority of the population of the target country as an attack on their independence rather than just the political leadership (Seyfi & Hall,

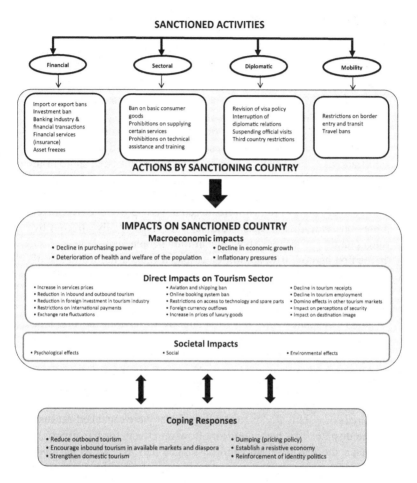

Figure 2.1 A conceptual model of the effects of sanctions on the tourism industry
Source: Seyfi & Hall (2019b)

2019a), as in the case of US sanctions against Cuba (see Box 2.2). This is illustrated in the case of the Qatar-Gulf crisis and the effects of sanctions by other Arab states on the Qatar tourism sector (Box 2.6).

As noted earlier, sanctions also usually have a disproportionate effect on the general populace, rather than the targeted government or persons. This has flow-on effects for outbound and domestic tourism as many of the affected are middle class people who are consumers of tourist services. For example, following EU and US sanctions against Russia's annexation of

Box 2.6 Qatar-Gulf crisis and Qatar tourism sector

Accusing Qatar for supporting terrorism and violating a 2014 agreement with the members of the Gulf Cooperation Council (GCC), four Arab nations (Saudi Arabia, Bahrain, UAE and Egypt) demanded that Qatar reduce diplomatic relations with Iran, stopping military coordination with Turkey, and closing Al-Jazeera. Qatar did not agree to any of these demands, which resulted in sanctions being imposed against Qatar in June 2017. These ranged from cutting diplomatic and trade ties with Qatar to banning Qatari airplanes and ships from utilizing their airspace and sea routes along with Saudi Arabia blocking the only land crossing. The ban on airspace use also meant that some Qatar Airways routes were affected leading to increased travel times on some flights. Qatar tourism was substantially affected by such punitive measures. About one million people visited the country in the first half of 2018, a third fewer than a year earlier with most of that decline coming from visitors from neighboring countries (Qatar Tourism Authority). Visitors from the Gulf Cooperation Council usually account for almost half of all visitors to Qatar.

Hotel occupancy rates declined slightly to 60% in the first half of 2018 compared to a year earlier. Revenue per available room fell 16% to 235 Qatari riyals ($65). Hamad International Airport, which had been positioning itself as a significant Middle-Eastern travel hub and is the home airport of Qatar Airways, suffered by a loss of about 27,000 passengers a day as a result of the air travel blockade, and hundreds of weekly flights to and from Qatar were cancelled because of the dispute. This had significant flow-on effects for the airport as it meant the loss of airline and passenger fees as well as terminal revenue from duty free shops and restaurants. It is estimated that air links suspended by the four Arab states represented around 25 percent of flights by state-owned Qatar Airways, one of the region's big three carriers. Elsewhere in the tourist sector, hotels, restaurants, and other facilities have had to find new sources of services and goods, in some cases at higher cost, due to the boycott.

The sanctions also affected the country's economic strategy as Qatar had identified tourism as one of five priority sectors for achieving economic diversification in Qatar. The development of business and leisure tourism is a key component of Qatar's drive to develop its economy away from reliance on oil and gas revenue with an aim to host five million visitors by 2023 and seven million in 2030 from a base of 1.8 million in 2018. In response to the sanctions Qatar eased restrictions on foreign investment, relaxed visa regulations, and sought partners to attract tourists from Russia, China, and India, as well as taking other measures to stimulate the sector. Furthermore, amid the ongoing political rift, Qatar also took punitive measures and stopped granting visas to Egyptian citizens seeking to enter the country.

Source: Adapted from the Middle East Eye (2017) and Sergie and Odeh (2018)

the Crimea, tourist flows from Russia to Europe have reduced (Ovcharov et al., 2015). The sanctions contributed to the substantial decline of the Russian ruble, impacted the image of Russia in tourism and investment terms, and contributed to the Russian financial crisis, which led to the decline of Russian operators in the tourist market. Similarly, in their study on tourism development in Serbia, Popesku and Hall (2004) noted that due to the economic sanctions then in place, Serbia became isolated from the international tourism market with long-term consequences along with regional and political change for the development of Serbian tourism.

The psychological and mental effects of sanctions lead to the creation of a negative image of a destination and increased perceived risk in certain markets, which also contributed to lower tourist arrivals (Pratt & Alizadeh, 2018). Countries exposed to sanctions are obliged to cope with the consequences of often being portrayed as international pariahs and destinations that are dangerous and/or unstable. This can then create a perception that visitors may be highly vulnerable and subject to local sensitivities on political matters, even though the on-the-ground reality for international visitors may be quite different (Seyfi & Hall, 2019a).

Social, cultural, and environmental issues are usually byproducts of economic sanctions. One of the clearest examples is the immediate and huge effects of sanctions on the purchasing power of ordinary people in countries exposed to sanctions, which can contribute to social and health problems. For example, there was a shortage of medicines following the tightening of sanctions on Iran in July 2012 (Moret, 2015). Due to the difficulties in importing technology under a sanction regime, many sectors with little to do with the military or even strategic interest, such as agriculture, can be affected, which can make it enormously difficult to pursue environmentally sound policies. Natural and cultural assets in countries exposed to sanctions are potentially open to harm as a secondary impact of sanctions. For example, with regard to the environmental dimensions, imposing sanctions means that the conservation and management of the cultural and natural heritage may suffer. Again, in the case of Iran, given the widespread sanctions on the country's central bank, Iran could not benefit from the UNESCO fund for the preservation and protection of its heritage (Seyfi et al., 2019). Due to the tense political relationship between Iran and the West and the negative image of Iran in international media, the country has also had difficulties in attracting international cooperation and expertise for inscription of its heritage sites (Seyfi et al., 2019). Furthermore, in a country subject to sanctions public spending priorities often change, and public resources shift to defense equipment and personnel to enhance the coercive capacity of targeted leadership and reinforce their leadership. As a result, other areas such as environment or production remain secondary while the focus is maintaining the ruling structure and sovereignty and ensuring regime survival (Brzoska, 2015).

Sanctions, coping responses, and tourism

Despite the widespread adoption of sanctions as a foreign policy instrument, knowledge as to how the sanctioned destinations respond to the sanctions to circumvent the effects on their political economy and how they deal with the effects of sanctions in a tourism context is surprisingly limited (Seyfi & Hall, 2019a). There is a paucity of information on which tools and resources sanctioned countries utilize to formulate policy responses to enable the country to adapt to the circumstances built by sanctions and to cushion the targeted sectors from the worst effects of sanctions. This information can provide important insights to understand how the political economy in these countries is reshaped in the light of economic and political uncertainty to minimize the effects of sanctions and is crucial to understanding the future trajectory of tourism under such a climate. Connolly (2018), for example, argues that while sanctions may cause some initial disruption, their impact on targeted sectors in the sanctioned country might quickly subside. But the likelihood of such an observation will be dependent on the length of time that sanctions are in place and their severity, as new institutions will be developed and economic trajectories reset the longer sanctions are in place.

Seyfi and Hall (2019a) argued that the dearth of knowledge on coping responses of sanctioned countries to sanctions may be related to the fact that, historically, countries subjected to sanctions are often neither a main tourism destination nor influential in terms of the global tourism generating market. However, recent sanctions on Russia and Turkey, two major actors in the global tourist system, may provide new perspectives on sanctions issues in relation to tourism.

Russia

In response to the Russian military intervention in Ukraine that began in 2014, international sanctions against Russia and Crimea were imposed by

Table 2.3 Restrictive measures imposed on Russia as a result of violations against Ukraine's territorial integrity

Restrictive measures	Type of sanctions
Asset freezes and visa bans on 132 persons and 28 companies or other entities in Russia/ Ukraine deemed responsible for the violation of Ukraine's territorial integrity	Asset freeze and travel ban
The suspension of preferential economic development loans to Russia by the European Bank for Reconstruction and Development (EBRD)	Financial
A ban on trading bonds and equity and related brokering services for products whose maturity period exceeds 30 days with some of Russia's biggest state-controlled banks (including Sberbank and Gazprombank), three Russian energy companies (including Rosneft, but not Gazprom in the case of the EU), and three Russian defence companies	Sectoral
A ban on loans to five major Russian state-owned banks	Financial
A two-way arms embargo	Arms embargo
A ban on exports of so-called dual-use items, i.e. civilian industrial goods that can be used as (or to produce) weaponry	Sectoral
A ban on exporting certain energy equipment and providing specific energy-related services to Russia's new, innovative and technology-intensive energy projects (e.g. Arctic and deep-water exploration, shale oil)	Sectoral

Source: Adapted from European Commission (2019) and OFAC (2019)

a large number of countries – including the USA and the EU – and several international organizations against individuals, businesses, and officials from Russia and Ukraine. As of August 2019, the sanctions continue to be in effect. The restrictive measures imposed on Russia are summarized in Table 2.3.

The sanctions contributed to the collapse of the Russian ruble and the Russian financial crisis (Dreyer & Popescu, 2014). In order to minimize the sanctions effects, Russia took several measures primarily by making a shift towards greater reliance on domestic resources – or 'Russification' – as a part of the securitization of strategic areas of economic policy on the one hand (i.e. import substitution and localization) and towards a more multi-directional foreign economic policy that emphasizes closer relations with non-Western countries, on the other (Connolly, 2018). The former shows that Russia has substantially emphasized greater investment in building domestic capabilities in targeted sectors (e.g. the energy, defense, and financial sectors as well as tourism), and the latter has been witnessed in the strategic and gradual shift of Russia towards new non-Western sources of technology and capital especially in Asia with an increasing focus on the members of the Shanghai Cooperation Organization (SCO). This also potentially has long-term implications for the development of new inbound markets as well as outbound travel. However, while these tactics might not necessarily be the most economically efficient solutions to Russia's economic challenges brought about by sanctions, they have helped to make Russia less vulnerable to external economic pressure including additional sanctions. Connolly (2018, p. 3) further explains that:

> The already considerable influence of the Russian state in key sectors of the economy proved to be particularly significant because it enabled the state to react in a relatively coordinated fashion to Western sanctions using a range of financial, institutional, and diplomatic measures.

The international sanctions on Russia represent an external political and economic shock that has had serious repercussions on the whole economy of the Russian Federation, including the tourism and hospitality industry (Ivanov et al., 2017). Reorienting from outbound to inbound tourism and using state-private partnerships to form, improve, and diversify domestic tourism products was one of the first responses of the Russian public sector towards the sanctions (Ovcharov et al., 2015). The Russian authorities also considered reinstating Soviet-style exit visas, which would severely limit Russians' right to travel abroad for the first time since the fall of the Soviet Union (Oliphant, 2015). Although the decline in personal incomes and revenues due to the economic crisis as a result of sanctions has pushed Russians to travel less abroad anyway. In the face of economic sanctions, the authorities have sought internal investment and the possibility of reducing the cost of imports. As a result, more attention was paid to domestic tourism. Under the 'import-substitution' and 'counter-sanctions' categories, certain restrictions on outbound tourism have emerged (establishing an exit visa), but also preferential policies for the domestic tourism sector and stimulation of consumer demand have been developed. Restrictions on outbound tourism and the ban on foreign companies from acting in the Russian tourist market have also become a factor in boosting domestic tourism. Overall, the reconstruction of the Russian tourism sector towards domestic tourism (increasing the share of domestic travel, promoting domestic travel and infrastructure development in Crimea) became one of the main objectives of circumventing sanctions for Russian tourism.

Private sector tourism and hospitality firms also responded in in order to maintain market share, which was increasingly vulnerable to internal, e.g. changed policy settings and external responses, e.g. changed perceptions of the Russian market, to the sanctions. Price discounts, season sales, and dumping were among the tactics that were used. Dumping is the selling of goods and services at prices lower than cost value. The large tour operators (Neva, Yuzhniy Krest, Labirint) all used dumping schemes (Ovcharov e t al., 2015). However, all four operators eventually went bankrupt, indicating that these tactics were only effective in the short-term to maintain market share. Such strategies were also a negative for the tourist market in general as they had a significant distorting effect on the development of various forms of organized tourism. Perhaps most significantly for the Russian travel sector the bankruptcies of the tour operators, which had previously been considered reliable, undermined the trust of consumers in the work of tour operators and travel agents and, as a result, many Russians have since stopped using the services of tourist agencies and begun organizing their own vacations (Ovcharov et al., 2015).

Iran

Iran has been the focus of sanctions by individual nations and international bodies since 1979 (Farahani & Shabani, 2013). Iran has been subjected to the largest and strongest sanctions regimes amid the nearly 8000 USA unilateral sanctions regime (Gilsinan, 2019) with the first sanctions imposed by the United States in November 1979 following the American Embassy hostage crisis. Since the early 1980s sanctions instruments have grown in their stringency (Takeyh & Maloney, 2011) with only a brief period from 2015 to 2018 in which the sanction regime was more limited. Table 2.4 shows the timeline of some the main international sanctions against Iran from their first imposition in 1979 following the hostage crisis to the more recent sanctions in President Trump' administration. Overall, the main aim of the sanctions' regime has been to reduce Iranian oil exports (which makes up over 80% of government budget) to zero as a part of a strategy to change Iran's behavior and to curb Iran's projection of regional power (Le Monde, 2018). However, different sanctions senders do have different strategies. For example, under the Trump administration the US has been focused on supporting Saudi Arabia and reducing Iran's regional influence as well as pushing for regime change. In contrast the EU has been more focused on encouraging Iran to the negotiating table as a means of managing its nuclear ambitions while also seeking to contain its involvement in Syria, Lebanon, and the Arabian Peninsula as well as its support for terrorist activities in Europe (Boogaerts, 2018).

Although Iran's landmark nuclear deal known as the *Joint Comprehensive Plan of Action* (JCPOA) achieved in 2015 could resolve a long-running dispute over Iran's nuclear enrichment program and nuclear ambitions, new sanctions were reintroduced following the United States' withdrawal from the nuclear deal with Iran in 2018 as part of an attempted strategy of regime containment and change. The tourism industry was one of the first areas of

Table 2.4 Timeline of main international sanctions against Iran

Year	Sanctioning actor	Types of sanctions
1979: Hostage crisis at the US embassy in Tehran (major turning point in Iran-US relations)		
1979	US	Asset freeze in US banks
1995	US	Total economic embargo
1996	US	Sanctions against foreign businesses investing in oil and gas
2002: The existence of secret nuclear sites in Iran is revealed		
2006	UN	Nuclear/ballistic missile program, freeze of financial assets, named individuals
2007	UN	Arms sales, financial assets
2008	UN	Assets for joint civilian-military use
	US	Ban on US banks taking intermediary role
2010	UN	Heavy weapons (tanks, missiles, fighter aircraft)
	EU	Oil sector, technology transfer, banking
2011	EU	Assets and specific individuals
2012	EU	Oil embargo, freeze of Iranian central bank's assets, ban on bank-to-bank transactions
2013	US	Ban on automobile sector and Iranian currency
		Ban on gold and petrochemicals
Nuclear deal of July 2015/suspensions and lifting of economic sanctions		
2018	US	US (May 2018) withdrawal from the nuclear deal and reimposition of sanctions including oil embargo; freeze of Iranian central bank's assets; ban on bank-to-bank transactions, gold, and petrochemicals; and wide-ranging US sanctions against Iran, including state bodies and individuals.
	EU	EU seeks to save nuclear deal by developing mechanisms to continue trade with Iran

Source: Seyfi and Hall (2018a)

the economy to witness an immediate growth in the light of the relaxation of sanctions against Iran in 2015 with Iran experiencing substantial growth in international tourism. More than five million inbound tourists visited Iran in 2017, nearly three times the number of 2009. In light of the easing of sanctions, European airlines such as Air France, British Airways, and Lufthansa and regional airlines, such as Air Asia, resumed direct flights to the country, and there was a considerable investment in tourism-related infrastructure (Khodadadi, 2016a; Seyfi et al., 2019). Yet, this period of relative prosperity for the tourism industry came to an end in the climate of rising regional tensions and the re-imposition of sanctions against Iran by President Trump's administration.

In response to the international stringent sanctions and as an overt policy response towards the sanctioning actors, Iran established what has been referred to as a 'resistive economy'. Historically, the term was first introduced in 2005 following the blockade of Gaza by Israel (Isaac et al., 2015) to describe attempts to maintain the regional economy. The term was then adopted in Iran by the leader of the country in 2010 as a response to toughened international sanctions imposed over Iran's economic lifeline oil exports along with restrictions on the international activities of the central bank (Smyth, 2016). Following the 2015 accord, interest in resistive initiatives was maintained as a result of the US not respecting the agreed terms of the nuclear agreement by not lifting financial sanctions, and it is still being emphasized in Iran given that the US withdrew from the nuclear deal.

The resistive economy is primarily intended to nullify the negative effects of Western sanctions and make Iran's economy more self-sufficient, especially via weaning the country off its heavy dependence on oil revenue through fiscal restraint, increased agricultural and manufacturing output, and strengthening the role of science in boosting technological innovation (Esfandiari, 2012). While the case for a resistive economy was initially developed to describe the situation brought about by sanctions, the term has now been stretched to also describe a near-siege wartime economy with low international trade or an economy with a vibrant private sector that can compete well internationally (Smyth, 2016). In the case of Iran, the concept of the resistive economy has taken on a different meaning more suited to its particular situation. Given the decades of sanctions, internal weaknesses, and the rentier economy, the Iranian economy remains little integrated in the international economic system, as evidenced by the very small amount of foreign direct investment received by Iran ($3.4 billion in 2016 according to the UN). Raising the standard of living (by growing the private sector and opening up the economy) while preserving social cohesion (by seeking to limit the rise of economic inequalities between social classes) are the two main economic objectives that the Iranian authorities have pursued. Coville (2018) argues that, in such a context:

> The resistive economy for Iran should mean that this country must find its own strategy of integration to globalization because it is clear that there is no other tactic that Iran could apply to achieve this integration. China has been successfully integrated into globalization since the late 1970s as it has defined and implemented its own strategy, based on a pragmatic approach of its strengths and weaknesses, without taking into account the economic liberalization models recommended at the time by the IMF or the World Bank.

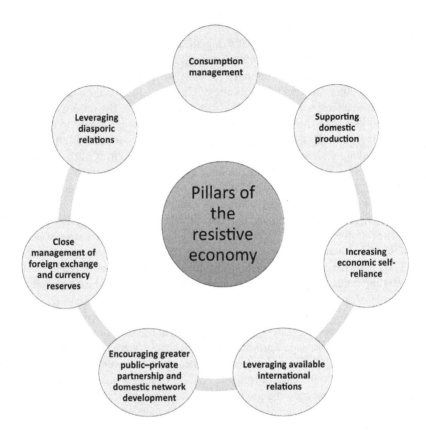

Figure 2.2 Conceptual model of the resistive economy

In general, resistive economic policies are aimed at reducing vulnerability to external economic pressures, including such events as the global financial crisis, along with supporting domestic production (Figure 2.2).

As shown in Figure 2.2, the resistive economy doctrine has a number of dimensions. This includes increasing energy security by lowering domestic energy consumption. In the Iranian case this is to be achieved by using the capacity of implementing targeted subsidies. It also aspires to achieve self-sufficiency in strategic products, such as food and medicine. Producing basic goods domestically can safeguard against sanctions by making them less vulnerable to reliance on international production chains. Provision of basic goods may also help prevent the domestic social unrest induced by economic challenges. In this regard, Iran has also sought to introduce various economic measures in an attempt to encourage domestic industrial activity.

However, a fundamental transition away from a state-dominated economy is sought by some Iranian policy actors in order to create the necessary space for private sector growth. As a continuation of resistive economy policy, the Iranian government plans to support locally-made products rather than importing foreign brands in an effort to reduce dependence on imports and foreign dollar-based currencies and build local capacity.

Ideas of greater economic self-reliance are also a significant part of security discourse (Tsygankov, 2002), as well as some strands of sustainable development thinking, including in a tourism context (Hall, Timothy, & Duval, 2004; Hall, 2002). Seyfi and Hall (2019a, p. 4) argue that:

> while the notion of the resistive economy builds on some of these strands of thought, it is very much a response to external political and, therefore, economic sanctions and constraints, rather than being an indigenous development that seeks to achieve socio-economic and environmentally progressive goals. Nevertheless, the extent of success or failure in implementing resistive economy measures in a tourism context has not been acknowledged in the literature, despite interest in the uses of tourism as a foreign policy measure and the inter-relationship between tourism and other policy fields.

In addition, the economy of resistance adopted by Iran in response to sanctions has been widely criticized. For example, economist Djavad Salehi-Isfahani (quoted in Le Monde, 2018) explains that:

> moderate Rohani's economic openness efforts could be "brutally interrupted" to give way to a "resistive economy", turned on its own, and tightly controlled by the authorities. The measures taken in recent weeks – exchange controls, rationing of foreign currencies, limitation of certain imports – all point in this direction.

Nevertheless, the degree of success or failure of the implementation of resistive economy measures in the context of tourism has not been addressed in the literature, despite the interest in tourism uses as a measure of foreign policy and the interrelationship between tourism and other policy areas (Seyfi & Hall, 2019a)

The resistive economy and sanctions

The resistive economy has substantial implications for the tourism industry in Iran as well as in similarly sanctioned countries. A major effect of sanctions is that the destination image of sanctioned countries and their promotion and attractiveness as a tourism destination is severely affected in some target markets. Three major resistive strategies appear to be utilized in response. First, the country can try to increasingly attract tourists from 'friendly countries' which, in the case of Iran, include Russia, China, and neighboring countries that may ignore American sanctions. As a response to American foreign policy and sanctions Iran is seeking to teach Russian at schools, rather than English, as strategic ties grow with Russia (Iran and Daily, 2018). Second, increased attention is given to attracting members of the diaspora, the size of which can be substantial, to return to visit family and friends and maintain contact with their heritage (VFR tourism in particular). Third, currency devaluation can be utilized as a means of encouraging more tourists to visit a 'cheap destination'. This latter strategy has become an important means of attracting visitors, especially in budget markets such as backpackers, who are also likely to be willing users of cheaper accommodation offerings as well as being interested in visiting regions outside of the major cities.

Sanctioned countries that seek to access international financial sources are forced into stronger financial relations with nations that remain friendly to it (Alipour & Kilic, 2005). Foreign investment from major Western hotel and restaurant chains is often restricted and investment in infrastructure may remain the domain of domestic firms or financial actors from friendly nations. Such a situation can also limit the opportunities for franchising and membership of international booking networks for sanctioned countries, which therefore also affects the level of integration in the international tourism information and distribution system. In the case of Iran, the development of new sets of financial relationships by Iran in Central and East Asia, China, and Russia has only served to strengthen tourism relations with these countries (Tehran Times, 2017). Diasporic investment may also be a significant alternative source of capital for the hospitality and tourism industry. Regardless, the overall strategy is to increase financial self-reliance and reduce dependence on foreign capital that may be susceptible to changed political and economic conditions.

Finally, the development of domestic tourism is a major focus of the resistive economy. Domestic travel can be encouraged directly by marketing campaigns and by imposing constraints on outbound travel, e.g. imposing limits on how much money can be taken out of the country and/or imposing a departure tax on outbound tourists that make outbound tourism more expensive. In the case of Iran, the government has tried to optimize tourism's contribution to the country's balance of payments, and domestic tourism has been given a great deal of attention and support so as reduce outbound flows (e.g. the introduction of a threefold rise in departure tax) (Box 2.7).

Box 2.7 Iran, sanctions and adaptation

Following the unilateral withdrawal of the US from the Iran nuclear deal in May 2018, new waves of sanctions were imposed on Iran. The aim of the sanctions is to exert 'maximum pressure' on Iran, thus depriving it of the revenues needed for financing, arming, and forming a vast network of regional allies (Seyfi & Hall, 2018c). In response, Iran is looking for ways around the US embargo, including ensuring that tourists continue to visit the country. With economic sanctions imposed by the US on almost every productive sector in Iran, the Iranian government hopes that World Heritage sites and other cultural and heritage attractions in the country, along with a range of other initiatives, will continue to attract tourists and their economic expenditure to Iran.

Iran has taken some protectionist measures to support the tourism sector in the face of the US sanctions. As a first step, the Iranian Tourism Organization (ICHTO), which is responsible for stimulating and coordinating national activities to develop tourism, has sought to ensure the continuation of foreign flights in the country despite the sanctions. A center responsible for making decisions on reducing the consequences of sanctions on the tourism industry has been created within this organization (Motamedi, 2019), and a number of coping mechanisms have been adopted:

Visa without stamp

To alleviate tourists' concerns over US sanctions on individuals who visit Iran, passports of travelers entering Iran are not being stamped. This policy is being made in response to US measures announced in 2017 that those visiting certain countries, including Iran, would face entry restrictions in the United States (Jalili, 2019). This policy has affected incoming tourism to Iran as tourists traveling to Iran may be afraid of sanctions, additional penalties, and not being able to travel to the United States after visiting Iran. This resulted in many travel cancellations to the country. With this new visa policy, foreign tourists are allowed to travel to Iran without having their passports stamped. The Iranian government believes this initiative can attract more tourists to Iran. A similar strategy is employed by Israel with respect to international arrivals. Israel no longer stamps tourists' passports (though it retains the right to do so). Visitors are instead given a small loose-leaf entry card to serve as proof of lawful entry thereby enabling the passport holder to more easily visit other countries in the Middle East.

Visa waiver policy for Chinese and regional travelers

Iran has put in place a visa-free policy for Chinese travelers, the world's largest outbound markets. Chinese citizens with a passport from the People's Republic of China or the Special Administrative Regions of Hong Kong or Macao can travel to Iran without a visa and can stay in the country for up to 21 days (Motamedi, 2019). The visa-free policy also reinforces the good trade relations between the two countries; Iran exports energy to China and Chinese state-owned enterprises invest in the Iranian oil and gas sector. The political climate has also become more conducive to strengthening ties between Iran and China given the economic policies of the administration of US President Donald Trump toward both countries. The lifting of visa restrictions is the first step in Iran's ambitious plan to increase the number of Chinese visitors from just over 50,000 in 2018 to two million by the end of 2020.

Departure tax

In order to reduce the outflow of foreign currency by outbound tourists, departure taxes were increased to around $60 for a single out-of-country trip from a fee of $20 in 2017. Subsequent trips over a 12-month period will incur even higher costs (Bezhan, 2017). Through this initiative the government hoped to limit Iranian spending abroad and boost domestic tourism by curbing outbound travel. Government officials also stated that part of the revenue from the tax increase would go towards developing tourism infrastructure and preserving cultural heritage sites. According to *The Financial Tribune* (2018a) after this initiative:

> The Iranian government has drawn 3 trillion rials ($24 million) from the departure tax in the first four months of the current year (March 21 to 22 July 2018). The figure indicates an increase of 177.2% over the same period last year, according to the latest data released by the Central Bank of Iran. Revenue from the departure tax, which is a sub-category of the goods and services tax and indirect taxes, is expected to hover around 2.7 trillion rials ($22 million) in a four-month period. The target for starting tax revenue gains for the current year is 8 trillion rials ($65 million).

Abolition of visa fees for tourists from neighboring countries

Strengthening infrastructure and cutting red tape are among the measures put in place to attract more visitors from countries in the region who are less affected by sanctions than Western tourists (Seyfi & Hall, 2018b). Iraqis are now exempt from paying visa fees to visit Iran. Through this initiative Iran hopes to further increase the number of tourists from Iraq, which is already the country's largest inbound tourist market, many of whom travel for religious and medical tourism as well as VFR. A total of 1,926,310 Iraqis visited Iran in 2018, followed by Azerbaijanis, Afghans, Turks, and Pakistanis (Seyfi & Hall, 2018b). Iran also exempted Azerbaijani tourists from visas while, as of October 2018, Omani nationals no longer require a visa or an entry stamp on their passport to enter Iran. Since 2018, Iran has announced numerous projects as part of its efforts to attract tourists from across the region with Egypt, Syria, Turkey, Lebanon, and Georgia being added to the list of countries whose nationals can obtain a visa upon arrival.

Visa upon arrival

Nationals of many countries who wish to travel to Iran can obtain a tourist visa upon arrival at Iranian airports. This system was put in place to better manage the flow of arriving travelers following growth in arrivals prior to the reintroduction of sanctions. All travelers, except nationals of the United States, the United Kingdom, Canada, Colombia, Somalia, Bangladesh, Jordan, Iraq, Afghanistan, India, and Sri Lanka, who are holders of an ordinary passport can, since 2015, obtain a 30-day tourist visa upon arrival in one of the many airports of the country (Seyfi & Hall, 2018b).

Religious tourism

The Iranian tourism administration has encouraged the arrival of Shiite pilgrims who visit the country and especially the religious cities. such as Mashhad or Qom. For example, Iran has strengthened its maritime tourism sector by activating several routes to attract more visitors to Iraq. Plans are underway to revive passenger shipping lines, including links between Iran and Saudi Arabia, Bahrain, Qatar, and Oman, as well as encourage rail link development (Financial Tribune, 2018b). Officials have announced plans to build a railway that starts in Khuzestan province in southwestern Iran, which crosses Iraq to the west and ends in the Syrian port city of Latakia. The three countries agreed to work together to develop the system in the hope of boosting religious tourism, as well as it having clear benefits for freight movement (Financial Tribune, 2018b).

Iranian diaspora

Migrant, diaspora, and VFR markets are among the least impacted by sanctions regimes. Iran benefits from its very large diaspora living abroad with numerous Iranians emigrating since the 1950s. There are no reliable and accurate statistics on the number of Iranians living permanently outside of Iran, although the estimate is between three and six million people. The largest population of Iranian emigrants, more than a million, live in the US. There are also smaller groups of Iranians in Canada, Europe, and the Gulf States (Sreberny & Gholami, 2016).

Health tourism

As a result of the reduction in the value of the Iranian currency, Iran has become a cheap destination for medical tourism and is positioning itself as a reliable and inexpensive destination for medical treatment, including organ transplantation, in China and India. Iran is already an important medical tourism destination, particularly with regard to eye and plastic surgeries for Iraqi, Omani, and Central Asian nationals. Although Western credit and debit cards, such as Mastercard and Paypal, do not work in Iran, the Iranian MahCard offers the possibility of transferring money from a foreign bank account to a debit card in Iranian currency in order to pay for medical treatment (Safaeian, 2019). The government is also devoting more resources to medical tourism by developing health tourism poles, particularly in Shiraz, the capital of Fars province in the south of the country.

Cryptocurrency

Iran is also developing a cryptocurrency in order to circumvent US sanctions (Fanusie, 2018), a strategy also attempted by Venezuela to counter international sanctions via its Petro cryptocurrency, whose value is indexed to the price of a barrel of Venezuelan oil ($60 at the time). It was created to allow Caracas to find fresh money in the markets while the United States prohibits anyone from buying Venezuelan oil under penalty of sanctions. Developing an Iranian cryptocurrency would potentially allow tourists to spend more easily by reducing barriers to access international payment systems. Due to international sanctions, the Iranian banking service is not part of the international banking service, and credit cards, including Visa or Mastercard, are useless in Iran. However, acceptance of any Iranian cryptocurrency might take many years as a result of perceptions of the risk and security surrounding such currencies in general.

Summary and conclusions

This chapter has examined how tourism has been directly and indirectly affected by sanctions. Sanctions were broadly categorized into four main types including financial, sectoral, diplomatic, and individual mobility sanctions. Each of these sanctions has different implications for tourists and the tourism industry at different scales. Overall, relatively little research has been conducted on sanctions in a tourism context despite their substantial impact on and relationship to tourism. This was seen as a function of both the growth of sanctions in the post-Cold War era as well as tourism not being recognized as a significant element in geopolitics or political economy until relatively recently. An additional element is that many of the countries against which sanctions have been placed are developing or transitional countries in which, while tourism is of substantial relative importance, do not constitute significant destinations in absolute numbers of tourists. Nevertheless, this was noted to have changed as a result of Russian sanctions on Turkey and US and EU sanctions on Russia.

The chapter provided a number of cases of sanctions, with their effects going beyond their immediate economic impacts to also have wider significance with respect to employment and social well-being. A useful concept to understand the responses of countries to sanctions was that of the resistive economy. Initially used in 2005 in Palestine with respect to the blockade of Gaza by Israel to describe attempts to maintain the regional economy, the term has since come to be adopted in Iran. A number of different resistive economy strategies against strategies were identified, with the encouragement of domestic tourism being an important factor in encouraging economic development along with reducing outbound tourism and attracting new markets and investment from countries that stay friendly to sanctioned regimes. However, the focus of this chapter has primarily been on state-to-state sanction relationships, while not ignoring the role of the state the next chapter identifies the important and perhaps growing role of consumer and interest group activism in tourism boycotts, a type of sanction that may require quite different responses to that of the resistive economy.

3 Boycotts and tourism

Introduction

While sanctions are a governmental tool to influence country, organization, and individual behaviors, boycotts have emerged as a consumer and interest group tool and as a form of 'economic voting' against the perceived unethical practices of companies and countries, which may or may not receive governmental support (Friedman, 1999; Klein, Smith, & John, 2004). To boycott is to refuse to purchase or use a product or service or take part in an activity as a way of expressing strong disapproval of a practice. In a tourism context it is usually associated with refusal to travel to a destination or attraction or use the services of particular companies. It may also be associated with the deliberate purchase of alternative products as acts of conscious consumption – what is otherwise referred to as a 'buycott' (Baptista, 2012). Both boycotts and buycotts are significant forms of political consumerism (Kelm & Dohle, 2018). Importantly, although many firms and countries will often claim that boycotts have little impact on them, independent research suggests that they do have some success (Gardberg & Newburry, 2009). In a study of 90 consumer boycotts Friedman (1999) found that 26.7% fully or partially achieved their objectives. Similarly, King (2008a, 2008b) found that 28% of the corporate targets in his study conceded to boycott demands.

Although different definitions of boycott exist, a clear understanding of the concept of tourism boycotts is lacking. There is only a relatively limited literature on tourism boycotts despite their substantial effects (Shaheer, Carr, & Insch, 2019). Where discussed, boycotts are often examined within the context and discourses of tourism crises (Glaesser, 2006; Henderson, 2007). More recently, Shaheer, Insch, and Carr (2018; Shaheer et al., 2019) have tried to provide insights into understanding how widespread tourism boycotts are and the reasons for boycotting tourist destinations.

Tourism has experienced a significant number of boycotts over time (Shaheer et al., 2018). Destinations, along with the tourism providers and attractions have been boycotted for deviating from perceived norms, which, at the destination level, have resulted in decreased arrivals and a negative destination image, at least in the short term (Gartner & Shen, 1992; Hudson, 2007; Van Rheenen, 2014). Boycotts have been sought for a variety of reasons including poor human rights records (e.g. Burma, China, South Africa, Saudi Arabia, Iran), treatment and policy towards LGBTs or minorities and communities (e.g. Mississippi and North Carolina case of anti-LGBT laws), violations of animal welfare and rights (e.g. Botswana and Namibia, Spain for bullfighting), and inappropriate environmental actions.

Depending on their level of consumer support boycotts may have direct, e.g. reduction in visitors, or indirect, e.g. negative image, adverse impacts on a destination, attraction, or a tourism service provider. Boycotts have the potential to decrease market share and sales and also damage the image of targeted companies and destinations (Shaheer et al., 2018) given that boycotts have been used by tourists as a means of expressing ethical concern and practice through their travel purchase decisions and use them as a form of punishment to coerce change in tourist destinations (Lovelock, 2012). For example, the destination boycott of Arizona over its controversial crackdown on illegal immigrants is estimated to have cost the tourism industry US$140 million (Gaynor, 2010a).

Shaheer et al. (2018) identified 146 destination boycotts that were initiated between 1948 and 2015, with more than 90% of the observed boycotts emerging between 2003 and 2015. They reported four main factors for the increasing number of boycotts over the years. [1] Innovation of new technology, specifically social media platforms such as Facebook and Twitter; [2] the increase in social movements; [3] emphasis on ethical consumerism; and [4] the use of tourism as a vehicle for social change. Shaheer et al. (2019) examined the reasons behind tourist boycotts and show that human rights violations (e.g. unjust treatment and policies towards the LGBT community or other discriminatory practices based on race, gender, and nationality; animal welfare concerns; and political and environmental issues are the most common reasons for destination boycotts. However, while the studies provide a useful indication of the scope of tourism boycotts it is difficult to gain an accurate assessment of boycott trends over time because of the availability of data and rapidly changing nature and scope of boycotting practices.

Boycotting: scope and understandings

Boycotting acts are often tied into organized collective public expressions of disapproval and protest thereby also potentially affecting the brand, image, and even commercial viability of the boycott target – a country, destination, government, individual, or firm – or combination thereof. Boycotts are among the most frequent forms of consumer expression against perceived unethical or egregious acts by firms and corporations (Farah & Newman, 2010) and are often regarded as a significant expression of political participation (Dalton, 2008). In some circumstances, pressure groups urge consumers not to buy specific products or the products of a particular business or country to pressure the latter to adopt ethical practices in its policy and behavior (Farah & Newman, 2010). This is of growing significance given its potential repercussions on corporate performance as well as the potential decrease of the market share and sales and damaging the image of targeted companies (Shaheer et al., 2018). Country or destination boycotts, of course, can affect individual businesses associated with specific countries and/or locations. Such boycotts may also receive the support of state or other institutions and may bear similarity to sanctions behavior with a key difference between the two actions being the extent to which they are incorporated under legislation. Losman (1972) argued that the imposition of a boycott against a country is a political act, designed to influence the practices and policies of the offending country by using utilizing economic weapons as the coercive force. Box 3.1 provides the example of the

---

Box 3.1 Arab League boycott of Israel

The Arab League, an umbrella organization comprising Middle Eastern and North African countries and entities (Egypt, Iraq, Jordan, Lebanon, Saudi Arabia, Syria, Yemen, Libya, Sudan, Morocco, Tunisia, Kuwait, Algeria, United Arab Emirates, Bahrain, Qatar, Oman, Mauritania, Somalia, Palestinian Authority, Djibouti, and Comoros. Syria is suspended as at the time of writing. Observer states include: Armenia, Brazil, Eritrea, India, and Venezuela), has maintained an official boycott of Israeli companies and Israeli-made goods and services since Israel was founded in 1948. The boycott is distinguished from a sanction as the Arab League does not enforce the boycott and boycott regulations are not binding on member states. Nevertheless, some member countries have enacted legislation to give force to the boycott. Egypt (1979), the Palestinian Authority (1993), and Jordan (1994) have treaties with Israel that have ended their participation in the boycott in full or in part, although individual consumers may still boycott Israeli products. Algeria, Mauritania, Morocco, and Tunisia do not enforce the boycott (Weiss, 2007).

The boycott consists of three tiers. The primary boycott prohibits citizens of an Arab League member from buying, selling, or entering into a business contract with either the Israeli government or an Israeli citizen. The secondary boycott extends the primary boycott to any entity world-wide that does business with Israel. The tertiary boycott prohibits an Arab League member and its nationals from doing business with a company that deals with companies that have been blacklisted by the Arab League. Enforcement of the boycott is relatively sporadic and appears dependent on the wider state of relations between Israel and Arab League countries, particularly over Palestine. Enforcement of the secondary and tertiary boycotts have decreased over time although Lebanon implements all three levels. The Gulf Cooperation Council (GCC) (Bahrain, Kuwait, Oman, Qatar, Saudi Arabia, and the United Arab Emirates) announced in 1994 that they would only enforce the primary boycott (Weiss, 2007).

> Despite the lack of economic impact on either Israeli or Arab economies, the boycott remains of strong symbolic importance to all parties. Many Arab countries want to deny normalization with Israel until there is a final resolution to the conflict in the Palestinian territories. Israel, on the other hand, asserts that it wants to be accepted in the neighborhood both in political terms and as a source of, and for, foreign investment.
>
> (Weiss, 2006, p. 7)

The US, itself a major user of sanctions as a foreign policy tool (see Chapter 2), has undertaken a range of legislative actions over time that aim to reduce the impact of the boycott. Most notably, Congress passed antiboycott legislation in the 1970s to discourage US individuals from cooperating with the secondary and tertiary boycotts. US antiboycott laws are included in the *Export Administration Act of 1979* and the Ribicoff Amendment to the *Tax Reform Act of 1976*. Although such legislation was designed to counteract the Arab League boycott, in practice, they apply to all non-sanctioned boycotts as they aim to prevent US firms from implementing foreign policies of other nations that run counter to US policy (Weiss, 2007).

The legislation makes it illegal for US companies to cooperate with the boycott and authorizing the imposition of civil and criminal penalties against US violators. US companies are required to report to the Department of Commerce any requests to comply with the Arab League Boycott. US taxpayers who cooperate with the boycott are subject to the loss of tax benefits that the US government provides to exporters. Section 535 of the *Foreign Operations, Export Financing, and Related Programs Appropriations Act, 2006,* states that (1) the Arab League boycott is an impediment to peace in the region and to United States investment and trade in the region; (2) the boycott should be revoked and the Central Boycott Office disbanded; (3) all Arab League states should normalize relations with Israel; and (4) the President and the Secretary of State should continue to oppose the boycott vigorously and encourage Arab states to assume normal trading relations with Israel (Weiss, 2007).

longstanding Arab League boycott of Israel as a case of a boycott that shares some similarities with sanctions, while it is also interesting because of the steps the US has set up to reduce the impacts of the boycott.

Boycotting decisions are increasingly used by consumers as an act of voluntary and intentional abstention from using, buying, or dealing with a person, organization, or country as an expression of protest, usually for ideological, moral, social, economic, political, environmental, or other reasons (Farah & Newman, 2010; Braunsberger & Buckler, 2011). At the same time that consumers support organizations with explicit environmental, societal, and political agendas they often also seek products and services that advocate or reflect particular positions on environmental, social, and political issues, e.g. Fair Trade, animal welfare, low-carbon, child-labor, chemical-free. Table 3.1 indicates some of the reasons for the undertaking of boycotts in a tourism context.

A boycott may be defined as 'the refusal and incitement to refusal to have commercial or social dealings with offending groups or individuals' (De Crespigny & McKinnel, 1960, p. 319). The *Encyclopedia Britannica* (2019) explains the historical origins of the term:

> The boycott was popularized by Charles Stewart Parnell during the Irish land agitation of 1880 to protest high rents and land evictions. The term *boycott* was coined after Irish tenants followed Parnell's suggested code of conduct and effectively ostracized a British estate manager, Charles Cunningham Boycott.

Friedman (1999, p. 4) describes a boycott as 'the attempt by one or more parties to achieve certain objectives by urging individual consumers to refrain from making selected purchases'.

Table 3.1 Examples of tourist boycotts

Category	Boycott target	Scale	Source
Animal welfare	Boycotting of Scottish tourism as a result of seal culls by fishing industry	Domestic, International	Parsons (2003)
Animal welfare	Boycott of Canadian seafood and other products, such as tourism, because of the Canadian seal hunt	International	Braunsberger and Buckler (2011)
Animal welfare	In 2002 in response to a proposed buffalo cull the Fund for Animals placed advertisements in *USA Today*, urging a tourist boycott of Montana: 'The State of Montana has a zero tolerance for buffalo, so we need you to have zero tolerance for Montana'	Domestic	Bidwell (2009)
Animal welfare	Pressure to conserve Loggerhead Turtles in Greece in order to avoid a tourist boycott campaign	International	Warren and Antonopoulou (1990)
Animal welfare & environment	Tourist boycott against the shooting of wolves in Alaska as part of a 'wolf control' program	Domestic	Regelin, Valkenburg, and Boertje (2005)
Environment	Tourist boycott of Victoria, Canada, in 1993 by Washington state because of the raw sewage Victoria was pumping into the shared Strait of Juan de Fuca	International	MacQueen (2005) and Alper (1997)
Environment	In the early 1980s environmental organizations in western Europe proposed a tourist boycott of Britain in response to the UK's emissions causing acid rain on the continent	International	Rosencranz (1986)
Inappropriate tourism development	Threat of tourist boycott if a private company built a tourist attraction where local fauna would be displayed behind plexiglass in Estes Park, Colorado (gateway to Rocky Mountain National Park)	Domestic	Wondrak (2002)
Human rights	Boycott of Guatemala organized by the International Union of Food and Allied Workers in 1979	International	Castaneda and Burtner (2010)

(Continued)

Table 3.1 (Continued)

Category	Boycott target	Scale	Source
Women's rights	Proposal that a scientific society should boycott New Orleans as a convention location because of Louisiana's strict abortion laws	Domestic	Barinaga (1991)
Worker rights & sexuality	Boycott of Disney by the Southern Baptist Convention because of a health benefits plan for employees in same-sex relationships, as well as perceived 'subliminal sexual messages' in *The Lion King*, and other entertainment regarded as inconsistent with 'family values'	Domestic	MacDonald and MacDonald (2014)
Politics	Boycotts of Olympic Games, including protests against apartheid South Africa; Russian invasion of Afghanistan; human rights in China; LGBT rights	International	Nafziger (1980), Keys (2018), and Sykes (2016)
Politics	US Jewish boycott of Mexico as a tourism destination following Mexico's support of 1976 UN resolution equating Zionism with racism and racial discrimination	International	Friedman (2004)
Politics	Development of Chinese mainland users of (censored) social media threat to boycott Hong Kong as a result of the Occupy Central campaign in Hong Kong	Domestic/ International	Luo and Zhai (2017) and Tolkach (2018)
Politics	Chinese threat of a tourist boycott unless Palau recognises the People's Republic of China rather than the Republic of China (Taiwan)	International	Chung-Min (2018)
Politics	Chinese tourist boycott of South Korea	International	Kim (2018)
Politics & human rights	Arab boycott of Israel since 1948	International	Turck (1976)
Politics & human rights	Cultural boycott of apartheid South Africa by African American artists	International	Freeman (2018)
Politics & human rights	Swedish tourist boycott of Spain as a result of General Franco's abuse of human rights	International	Lilljegren (2016)
Politics & human rights	Boycott of products of US companies in Jordan as a protest against US policies on Palestine and Israel	Intermestic	Kilani (2003)

Category	Boycott target	Scale	Source
Politics & human rights	In 1987 the governor of Arizona rescinded an executive order issued the previous year that established a holiday in honour of the slain civil rights leader, Dr. Martin Luther King, Jr. This led to a major convention boycott	Domestic	Teye and Diffenderfer (1988)
Politics & human rights	Calls for boycott of the Sydney Olympics because of Australia's policies towards Aboriginals	Domestic	Waitt (2001)
Politics & human rights	Tourist boycott of Myanmar in the 1990s	International	Bray (2002)
Policing	In the mid-1990s following perceived inaction after a US girl went missing in Aruba there were calls for a tourist boycott	International	L'Etang, Falkheimer, and Lugo (2007)
Imprison-ment & conviction	Public campaign for a tourist boycott of Bali by supporters of a convicted Australian drug-runner to assist her early release	International	Richardson (2005)

According to Klein et al. (2004), boycotts are an extreme case of a broader category of consumer behavior in which social and ethical issues influence purchase decisions. Garrett (1987, p. 47) sees a boycott as:

concerted, but non-mandatory, refusal by a group of actors (the agents) to conduct marketing transactions with one or more other actors (the target) for the purpose of communicating displeasure with certain target policies and attempting to coerce the target to modify those policies.

Another useful approach towards the concept of a boycott is from John and Klein (2003, p. 1198) who define a boycott as occurring when

a number of people abstain from purchase of a product, at the same time, as a result of the same egregious act or behavior, but not necessarily for the same reasons. Following Smith (1990), we refer to a boycott as "effective" if there is nonzero participation, and "successful" if the boycott leads to the cessation of the egregious act. The egregious act is a source of disutility to individuals, either directly (for example, adverse health effects from a polluting firm) or vicariously (for example, the negative emotions that stem from envisioning a firm's use of child labor).

	Target of boycott	
	Direct	**Indirect** Target is surrogate for the actor whose actions are objectionable
Instrumental boycott Aims to coerce the actor whose actions and/or policies are objectionable to change a disputed policy	The Boycott, Divestment, Sanctions (BDS) campaign against Israel Chinese threat of a tourist boycott unless Palau recognises the People's Republic of China rather than the Republic of China (Taiwan)	Boycott of products of US companies in Jordan, including hotel chains, as a protest against US policies on Palestine and Israel
Purpose of boycott **Expressive boycott** Communicates firm or consumer displeasure with the actions and/or policies of the actor	Swedish tourist boycott of Spain as a result of General Franco's abuse of human rights Tourist boycott of Myanmar in the 1990s	Boycott of Canadian seafood and other products, such as tourism, because of the Canadian seal hunt

Figure 3.1 A categorization of boycotts

Figure 3.1 presents a means of categorizing the target of boycotts on the basis of purpose, instrumental or expressive in relation to the actor whose actions are so objectionable so as to warrant a boycott and as to whether the target is affected directly or indirectly. It is important to distinguish between the target of a boycott and the actor whose actions are objectionable. In many (direct) cases these are one and the same. However, in other (indirect) situations the target acts as a surrogate for the actor whose actions are objectionable. An example of this type of situation is where what are regarded as American companies, franchises, or brands are seen by boycotters as surrogates for US policy and actions, something which may be extremely significant in the lodging and hospitality sectors. Ettenson and Klein (2005) suggest that, 'indirect boycotts are often triggered by a controversial international event: the policies and actions of a foreign country are objectionable to a group of consumers and the ensuing protest is visibly played out in the international marketplace'. An example being the boycotting of Air France as a protest against French nuclear testing in the South Pacific in the 1980s and 1990s. Box 3.2 provides a similar, more recent case of indirect boycotts, with the example of Korean consumer and business boycotts of Japanese goods and tourism. Direct tourism boycotts tend to occur at a destination level or at the level of the firm,

Box 3.2 Korean boycott of Japanese goods and tourism

Trade and historical tensions between Japan and South Korea expanded into a boycott of Japanese goods and services in 2019. Anti-Japanese feelings in Korea grew following Japan's decision on 1 July 2019 that it would restrict exports of materials used in the manufacture of semi-conductors, which is a major industry and employer in Korea. A later announcement also saw the formal reduction of intelligence sharing with respect to North Korea between the two countries. A range of individual and collective responses emerged. Sales of Japanese beer in Korea were reported to be down as much as 40% in mid-July, summer in Korea, with sales of other imported beer rising. However, convenience store chain CU reported sales of Korean beer had grown only 2.8% over the period, suggesting, as Blair (2019) noted, that 'even patriotism had its limits'. From a tourism perspective, bookings for trips to Japan fell by up to 70%, while travel agents reported that almost half of previously booked holidays were being cancelled.

Some members of the Korea Oil Station Association homepage, which operates petrol stations and garages, called for petrol stations to refuse to serve customers driving Japanese cars, while on 19 July an alliance of garages announced it would not repair cars from Japan However, some media were concerned that the campaign was setting Korean against Korean. The online news outlet *E Today* stated

> A war can never be won if we don't know if those we are shooting at are our friends or enemies. . . . The victim of the gas stations refusing to fill up Japanese cars isn't the Japanese government but the car owners. If people don't use gas stations, the victim is not the Japanese government but the gas station owners.
>
> (quoted in Blair, 2019)

Another target was the Japanese anime film *Butt Detective the Movie*, a spin-off from a popular anime series featuring a detective with a head shaped liked a bottom, which was targeted by online posts calling for a boycott on Japanese films. According to a representative for the film's Korean distributor 'We are currently reducing promotional marketing or events to meet public sentiment and taking public interest into account' (Korea Biz Wire quoted in Blair, 2019).

Source: Blair (2019)

e.g. businesses who are seen to have inappropriate human rights and labor rights records (Zapata Campos, Hall, & Backlund, 2018). Delacote (2009) distinguishes between market boycotts and media-oriented boycotts, the aim of which is to signal disapproval and to increase public awareness, although this categorization seems extremely artificial given the role that media play in influencing consumer perceptions of products, companies, and brands.

Friedman (1991, 1999) identified instrumental and expressive purposes for boycotts. An instrumental policy aims to change a target's actions or policies. For example, in the US the Southern Baptist Convention and some other socially conservative Christian groups campaigned to boycott Disney because of their corporate health benefits plan for employees in same-sex relationships, as well as perceived 'subliminal sexual messages' in films like *The Lion King*, and other entertainment that were not regarded as consistent with the groups' notions of 'family values' (MacDonald & MacDonald, 2014). In contrast, expressive boycotts 'are a more generalized form of protest that communicates consumers' displeasure with the actions of the target. Typically, this form of protest is characterized by a vague statement of goals and may simply vent the frustrations of the protesting group' (Ettenson & Klein, 2005, p. 201) and individuals (see Box 3.3). As such a

---

Box 3.3 Customers call for boycott of Equinox and SoulCycle

SoulCycle is a boutique fitness brand in the US and the UK that combines stationary cycling with motivational talks from instructors, along with candle-lit rooms and high-end music equipment. In August of 2019 customers of the fitness companies Equinox and SoulCycle took to social media to call for a boycott of the brands after news that a high-profile billionaire investor, Stephen Ross, would be hosting a fundraising event for President Donald Trump. Ross, who is also the owner of the NFL team the Miami Dolphins, is the chairman of Related, the company that owns Equinox Fitness which, in turn, has a 97% stake in SoulCycle. In response to the social media backlash against the fundraising event, the CEO of SoulCycle Melanie Whelan released a statement addressed 'To Our Soul Family'. Whelan said the company has 'nothing to do with the event and does not support it. . . . We're committed to all our riders and the communities we live in. Mr Ross is a passive investor and is not involved in the management of SoulCycle.' However, Twitter and other social media users responded that Ross was more than a 'passive investor' and furthered calls for customers to quit SoulCycle and Equinox.

Source: Aratani (2019)

boycott may be an end in itself. Importantly, the 'same' boycott may have features of both instrumental and expressive purposes. For example, the boycott of international tourist visitation to Burma/Myanmar in the 1990s or apartheid South Africa in the 1970s and 1980s had instrumental (organized protest and lobby groups) as well as expressive (more general recognition of the inappropriateness of visitation because of the governing regimes) elements (Hall & Ringer, 2000; Bray, 2002).

Boycotts have been examined through a number of different disciplinary and subject lenses, including sociology and history (Caruana, 2007, Laidler, 1913; Hyman, 1980; Friedman, 1991); psychology and economics (Hahn & Albert, 2017; Mahoney, 1976; Gardberg & Newburry, 2009; Sen et al., 2001; Klein et al., 2004); political science (Endres & Panagopoulos, 2017; De Crespigny, & McKinnel, 1960; Stolle, Hooghe, & Micheletti, 2005); marketing (Koku, 2012; Garrett, 1987; Klein et al., 2004); and tourism (Kilani, 2003; Parsons, 2003; Henderson, 2007; Olson & Park, 2018; Shaheer et al., 2018, 2019). Garrett (1987), like many who approach boycotts from a public policy or political science perspective, argues that boycotts involve a simultaneously 'organized' effort – by a single group or by a number of groups, which may include state institutions – to force a target to modify its policies. However, as Ettenson and Klein (2005) suggest, although this characterization of boycotts is appropriate in many circumstances, it overlooks the role of individual-based behavior in marketplace protests and argue that a focus on individual-based boycott behavior is significant for three reasons.

1 although a single or group of organizations may call for a boycott, the success or failure of the action largely depends on an individual's willingness to participate;
2 consumers can have different motivations for participating in the common action of a boycott (Sen et al., 2001; John & Klein, 2003). As Ettenson and Klein (2005, p. 202) note 'Some may desire to change the actions of the target (instrumental motivations), while others may choose to participate simply to express their indignation (expressive motivations). A single individual might boycott for both instrumental and expressive reasons'; and
3 an individual may decide to participate in a boycott as a form of protest that is independent of any direct affiliation with a formal organization.

Given that individual decision-making is so critical for the success of boycotts, particularly in a tourism context where boycotts are usually predicated on not travelling to a specific destination or purchasing a product from a particular firm, the next section of this chapter looks at the individual scale and consumer motivations for participating in boycotts, before moving on to the impact of different boycotting examples.

Consumer motivations for boycott participation

There has been growing research on an individual consumer's motivation to boycott products and services. A number of motivations for boycott participation have been suggested: collective effort for behavior change (Friedman, 1999); a complex emotional expression of individuality and a vehicle for moral self-realization (Kozinets & Handelman, 1998); an expression of outrage for self-esteem maintenance, or even enhancement (Brewer & Brown, 1998); preserving a sense of belonging (Sen et al., 2001); and a sense of moral obligation (Farah & Newman, 2010).

Friedman (1999) argues that when consumers participate in boycott practices they are actuated by two types of motives: instrumental and non-instrumental (see also Figure 3.1). An instrumental motivation aims to pressure the target to change a disputed policy. In contrast, a non-instrumental motivation is a more generalized form of objection to communicate consumer dissatisfaction towards the actions of their target. While being complex in the reality, it is also argued that the majority of people who boycott only concentrate on the instrumental dimension whereby consumers weigh the perceived costs and benefits of participating in a boycott (Nguyen, Ngo, Ngo, & Kang, 2018). However, the motivation to participate or not participate in boycotting behavior cannot simply be seen as an effort to gain collective benefits or avoid personal costs – instrumental motivation – but rather is also often influenced by individual emotional elements – non-instrumental motivations (Makarem & Jae, 2016; Friedman, 1995, 1999). Thus, showing that boycotting is a way for consumers to emotionally express themselves in boycott behavior even though the actual target may not be the actor that is actually engaging in the disapproved action or policy (see Box 3.2 with respect to South Korean consumer boycotts of Japanese products and tourism). In a Greek study of the possibility of boycotting a hotel due to unethical practices, Tilikidou, Delistavrou, and Sarmaniotis (2013) found that almost all respondents declared their intentions to boycott hotels accused of environmental damage and unethical labor practices. Respondents did not seem to take the type of ownership (local or foreign) of any given hotel into consideration. Consumers who were most likely to boycott environmentally sustainable hotels were older than 34 years of age and retired persons. Customers were also influenced by their past boycotting experience. Where no unethical issues occurred, price was an important factor in the decision making process over hotel selection.

There are also some restraining factors of incentive to participate in boycotts. (i.e. the costs associated with the consumer's dependence, preference, and/or loyalty to the boycotted product (John & Klein, 2003), as well as the unavailability in the marketplace of affordable substitutes (Sen et al.,

2001). Hahn (2018) explains two fundamental reasons for such absenteeism in boycott participation. First, the small agent problem, where consumers may feel that their individual participation will make no difference to the situation. 'By participating in a boycott, the consumer must bear the cost of the boycott (the foregone consumption of the boycotted product). However, the benefit of the boycott – changing the unethical behavior of the target firm – is not in the hands of the individual consumer' (Hahn, 2018). Second, the free-rider problem, in which individual consumers let others bear the cost of boycotting. 'While boycotts require widespread participation to be effective, the small agent and free-rider problems undermine the incentive of individual consumers to participate in boycotts. Eventually, this leads to a downward spiral. The fewer consumers who participate in a boycott, the less the chance of success – which further lowers the attractiveness of participating' (Hahn, 2018). However, despite such economic framing of the boycotting issues there remain people who boycott, even if they are aware of the likelihood that their action or protest will potentially make no difference because it remains the 'right thing' to do and who treat boycotts and buycotts as an ethical decision. Indeed, over time the consequences of such ethical decisions with respect to consumption can become substantial. For example, the hospitality sector is increasingly having to respond to the ethical concerns of vegans and others who have made the ethical decision to boycott products taken from animals (Sapontzis, 2004; Freeman, Bekoff, & Bexell, 2011) as well as issues of animal, climate, human, and environmental welfare in their supply chain.

Consumers also seem to be increasingly more aware of their role as citizens in society through their political engagement in social networks (Loader, Vromen, & Xenos, 2014). This is seen in various practices including political consumerism (Micheletti & Stolle, 2008), consumers' attachment to ethical concerns (Irving, Harrison, & Rayner, 2002; Chatzidakis & Lee, 2013), and by consumers seeking to be heard by companies turning the communication process, which often seemed to be unidirectional – from companies to consumers, into a two-way process (McGriff, 2012). The latter is of significance given the potentially strong empowerment of consumers via social media practices and the vulnerability of some companies and brands to negative publicity. However, both consumer empowerment and the susceptibility of companies to boycotts need to be understood as uneven. For example, some types of products and their associated certification schemes are more successful than others. Where they are successful it appears to be grounded in:

1   being easily traceable allowing provenance to be established;
2   the visibility and tangibility of the product to consumers;

3   the economic value of consumer purchase; and
4   the symbolic value of the product, with any negative association destroying or reducing its value.

(Nielsen & Gibbon, 2011)

The contemporary political, social, and environmental justice movements also highlight the emergence of alternatives to boycotts from consumer-based advocacy campaigns (Box 3.4). For example, the buycott, also sometimes referred to as a positive boycott or anti-boycott, has emerged as a strategy to influence and reward firm behavior. In tourism, although not necessarily always stated as such, the notion of a buycott is best seen in the

---

Box 3.4   Corporate critic: Ethical Consumer Research Association

Ethical Consumer is a not-for-profit UK magazine and website founded in 1989 which publishes information on the social, ethical and environmental behavior of companies and issues around trade justice and ethical consumption (2019). The mission of the Ethical Consumer Research Association (ECRA) is to promote 'a society where the environment is respected, where human rights are properly protected and where animals are no longer cruelly exploited' (2019). Corporate Critic is a product of the ECRA that indexes and rates the CSR of over 25,000 publicly listed and private companies from around the world. Information is collected and categorized in five main areas:

- Environment: climate change, pollution and toxics, habitats and resources, environmental reporting, nuclear power;
- People: human rights, workers' rights, supply chain policy, irresponsible marketing, armaments;
- Animals: animal testing, factory farming, other animal rights;
- Politics: genetic engineering, boycott call, political activities, anti-social finance, company ethos; and
- Product sustainability: organic product, Fairtrade product, positive environmental features, other sustainability features, animal welfare.

Source: Corporate Critic. Ethical Consumer Research Association (2018)

development of ecolabels and other sustainability labels to encourage consumer purchase (Howard & Allen, 2010), although at a destination level the notion of consumer nationalism potentially becomes important in promoting domestic and diasporic forms of tourism (Castelló & Mihelj, 2018). A blend of the two approaches is perhaps seen in 'buy local' campaigns, which merge promotion and labelling and concerns over supply chains with 'local patriotism', and which is best seen in the focus of some restaurants, hotels, and markets on the promotion of local food. While boycotts and buycotts share many similarities, they are different is some ways, as explained by Pezzullo (2011, p. 125):

> . . . A *boycott campaign* is a concerted refusal to spend money as well as to convince others to refuse to spend money on a product or service in the hopes of changing specific condition(s) or practice(s) of an institution. In contrast, a *buycott or procott or girlcott* campaign is a concerted effort to make a point of spending money as well as to convince others to make a point of spending money on a product or service in the hopes of affirming specific condition(s) or practice(s) of an institution.

Both boycotts and buycotts highlight the need for tourism and hospitality businesses and destinations to develop better coping marketing and communication strategies. Interestingly, in a study of 1,023 boycott events with 93 targeted firms in Korea during 2006–2016, Yang and Rhee (2019) found that public boycotts positively affected CSR disclosure speed, although the disclosure speed did also vary depending on the magnitude of the potential loss resulting from failing to act and from simply responding too slowly to such boycotts. Nevertheless, CSR disclosure was found to be a significant risk-reduction mechanism against boycotts given greater transparency with respect to business policies and actions. Such a finding was also in keeping with Gardberg and Newburry's (2009) analysis of more than 25,000 individual evaluations of 59 companies which suggested that individuals are less likely to boycott companies about which they are knowledgeable.

Several empirically-based studies have found increases in participation in boycotts over time (Stolle et al., 2005 [USA]; Listhaug & Grønflaten, 2007 [Norway]). However, there are limited estimates of the extent of participation in boycotts and buycotts that make it difficult to generalize beyond specific countries and regions, demographics or even samples. Data from the World Values Survey of Inglehart et al. (2014) does suggest that there has been an increase in boycotting behavior over the period from 2005 to 2015 although substantial caution needs to be had with respect to sample size (Table 3.2). Nevertheless, the data does seem to illustrate the significance of boycotts in countries such as Thailand, as well as in a number of

Table 3.2 World Values Survey. Political action recently joined in: boycotts. 2005–2009 vs 2010–2014

Country	Have done		Not done/not at all		Don't know/no answer/ missing		N	
	2005–2009	2010–2014	2005–2009	2010–2014	2005–2009	2010–2014	2005–2009	2010–2014
Australia	10.3%	54.5%	87.2%	35.2%	2.5%	10.0%	1 421	216
China	3.8%	30.5%	94.4%	9.0%	1.8%	60.5%	1 991	164
Germany	5.6%	49.1%	91.6%	48.7%	2.8%	2.2%	2 064	265
India	12%		67.1%		20.8%		2 001	
Netherlands	11.1%	31.4%	76%	4.0%	10.3%	64.6%	1 050	1 902
New Zealand		42.8%		43.3%		13.9%		201
Slovenia	4.5%	18.9%	93%	73.7%	2.5%	8.4%	1 037	275
South Africa	8.2%	48.9%	90.3%	23.6%	1.4%	3.5%	2 998	292
Sweden	17%	47.6%	70.6%	50.6%	0.3%	1.8%	1 003	264
Thailand	3.1%	85.3%	96.7%	11.5%	0.3%	3.2%	1 534	157
USA	18.4%	56.9%	78.5%	42.2%	3.1%	0.9%	1 249	346
Total	8.8%		86.1%		5.1%		16 332	

World Values Survey selected samples: Australia 2005, 2012; China 2007, 2013; Germany 2006, 2013; India 2006; Netherlands 2006, 2012; New Zealand 2011; Slovenia 2005, 2011; South Africa 2006, 2013; Sweden 2006, 2011; Thailand 2007, 2013; United States 2006, 2011.

Question wording: Have you or have you not done any of these activities in the last five years? (Read out and code one answer for each action): joining in boycotts

Source: Derived from Inglehart et al. (2014)

western countries. Table 3.3 also illustrates the frequency of boycotting, with Thailand, Australia, and Sweden all having over 15% of respondents from those countries saying that they had engaged in a boycott more than three times in the past five years.

In the European context Gallego (2007) found an enormous variation of participation in boycotting behavior, with Sweden having the highest percentage (34.8%), followed by Finland (29.3%) and Denmark (28.3%), and Ukraine (1.8%), Portugal (2.1%) and Slovenia (2.2%) having the lowest. Dalton (2008), who reported that in 2005 18% of Americans stated that they had boycotted a product for political or social reasons in the previous year, and 22% said they bought a product for such reasons. Such figures also suggest that boycotting behavior is also related to political cultures and structures. In Gallego's (2007) analysis of European social survey data found that women only took part more frequently in three Nordic countries and in Germany, while in Greece they are less likely to do so. Educational level was found to be the only widespread determinant of participation in boycott activities on a country basis, although at an aggregate European level the coefficient for income was even greater than that of education.

Human rights violations and tourism boycotts

In the analysis of Shaheer et al. (2019) of reasons for boycotting tourist destinations with 146 boycotts identified in 76 countries, human rights violations were regarded as the most common reason for a destination being boycotted, forming nearly half of the boycotts analyzed. Tourism boycotts of destinations with poor human rights records are used as a tool by potential visitors or even repeat visitors to punish these destinations, potentially having an adverse impact on the destination. Boycott of tourist destinations for their human rights concerns have been related to two main groups: unjust treatment and policies towards the LGBT community and discriminatory practices based on race, ethnicity, or nationality.

Given anti-LGBT laws and hostility in some destinations toward LGBT, many people have challenged the morality of traveling to destinations that are perceived to be anti-LGBT or have clear anti-LGBT policies in place and asked for their boycott, e.g. boycott of North Carolina for its anti-LGBT policies, or boycotting Sochi Olympics for Russia's anti-LGBT policy. Many LGBT people base their travel destinations on the perception of which destinations are the most LGBT friendly (see Box 3.5). This is economically significant for many destinations as in 2016 the LGBT community's buying power was estimated to be approximately $917 billion and much of that represented by older Millennials, GenXers, and Baby Boomers. US LGBT

Table 3.3 World Values Survey 2010–2014. Political action recently joined in: Boycotts. Frequency of boycotting

Frequency of boycotting	%	Aust.	China	Germ.	Neth.	NZ	Slov.	SA	Sweden	Thai.	USA
Not at all	23.6	35.2	9	48.7	4	43.3	76.7	23.6	50.6	11.5	42.2
Once	28.8	27.5	19.9	22.4	31.4	32.3	10.9	28.1	22.4	44.3	34.7
Twice	5.9	9	7.6	9.2	0	6.5	2.5	27.6	5.3	16.7	12.1
Three times	1.9	2.8	0.6	5.4	0	1	0.4	8.6	3.6	4.5	3.5
More than three times	4.9	15.5	2.5	12.1	0	3	1.1	8.6	16.2	19.9	6.6
Don't know	0.5	0	0	2.2	0	0	0.4	3.5	1.4	0	0
No answer	34.5	10	60.5	0	64.6	13.9	8	0	0.4	3.2	0.9
(N)	4082	216	164	265	1902	201	275	292	264	157	346
Mean	2.01	2.29	2.18	2.08	1.89	1.7	1.23	2.49	2.11	2.76	1.97
Standard deviation	1.12	1.45	1.01	1.39	0.32	0.92	0.63	1.21	1.48	1.32	1.14

World Values Survey elected samples: Australia 2012; China 2013; Germany 2013; Netherlands 2006, 2012; New Zealand 2011; Slovenia 2011; South Africa 2013; Sweden 2011; Thailand 2013; United States 2011.

Question wording: Have you or have you not done any of these activities in the last five years? (Read out and code one answer for each action): joining in boycotts

Source: Derived from Inglehart et al. (2014)

Box 3.5 LGBT inclusiveness and the impact of religious freedom laws

LGBT (lesbian, gay, bisexual, and transgender) tourism accounts for more than an estimated 6% of the global tourism market (Ram, Kama, Isaac, & Hall, 2019). The potential economic significance of the LGBT tourism market has attracted the attention of many destination marketing organizations and tourism businesses, accentuating the perception of the LGBT community as a lucrative market, while also indicating the special needs of the LGBTs, especially concerning their need for inclusion and feelings of safety (Pritchard, Morgan, Sedgley, Khan, & Jenkins, 2000; Puar, 2002).

Religious Freedom Laws (RFL) that are aimed at prohibiting laws that burden a person's freedom of religion, e.g. by allowing people to refuse a particular product or service to consumers on the basis of their religion such as flowers or cakes for a LGBT wedding, have become a source of contention in Australia and the United States (Webster, Yen, & Hji-Avgoustis, 2016). Drawing on boycott literature, Olson and Park (2018) tested a structural model involving five constructs: egregiousness, LGBT support, self-enhancement, boycott, and destination image on a sample of 306 respondents. Their findings indicate two paths, direct and indirect, to boycott decisions from perceived egregiousness. Their results suggest that boycott decisions in terms of RFL were determined by individual tourists' perceptions of the egregious act and the intrinsic rewards of self-enhancement from supporting the LGBT movement. In addition, boycott decisions led to a negative image of a destination. Olson and Park (2018) also received a degree of support from Ram et al.'s (2019) research in Tel Aviv, which found that the inclusive policy by the Tel Aviv Municipality raised positive attitudes among all tourists, not only the LGBT community. Indeed, gay-friendliness was even found to mitigate the perceived risks associated with terrorist attacks. The research of Olson and Park (2018) and Ram et al. (2019) therefore reinforces that LGBT friendliness is an important function in the construction of a positive city or location image.

Source: Olson & Park (2018) and Ram et al. (2019)

citizens alone account for over $200 billion for LGBT leisure spending globally (Forbes, 2018).

The significance of human rights issues as a major dimension of tourism related boycotts should perhaps not be surprising given that marginalization has been recognised as a factor driving boycotting (Gardberg & Newburry, 2009). Marginalization implies 'instability, expendability, lack of power, and an absence of full integration with centralized decision-making' (Arnold, 1995, p. 88). Types of marginalization include – but are not limited to – economic, political, social, and cultural marginalization, each characterised by a lack of resources. Economic marginalization tends to affect minority racial, cultural, or ethnic groups, the elderly, youth, and single mothers (Gardberg & Newburry, 2009). According to Cruz (2017, p. 9), minority boycotts are featured as:

> Actions undertaken by a minority group (when related to society as a whole or other consumers) who has his own objectives or circumstances when compared with the majority rest, or, still, pro groups in vulnerable position (e.g. racial or homosexual segregation context).

One of the most well-known examples of boycotts for human rights violations was the worldwide boycott of the apartheid regime in South Africa. Individual boycotting of South African products during the apartheid era was matched by UN and government imposed trade sanctions together with sporting and cultural boycotts, which sought to dissuade sports teams from travelling to the country and entertainers from performing. As a consequence of boycotts and sanctions, international tourist arrivals in South Africa sharply declined from one million in 1980 to 290,000 in 1986 (Pile, 2018).

Another example is the Myanmar (formerly known as Burma) boycott for its poor human rights record during authoritarian military rule (Pedersen, 2013). More recently, the widespread wave of international outrage in response to the forced mass exodus of the Rohingya from Rakhine state again challenged the ethicality of visiting Myanmar (Kemp, 2017; Tajuddin, 2018). A potential new tourism boycott of Myanmar has been subject to debate. One view believes that a tourism boycott would have little impact on the government while adversely impacting ordinary people involved with tourism activities and whose livelihood is dependent on tourism. Others argue that given the degree of government involvement in the country's tourism industry, e.g. airlines and the tax revenue raised via tourism a boycott may influence the regime's actions. However, the history of economic sanctions against Myanmar shows that sanctions were not successful and did not have a substantial contribution to a democratic transition in Myanmar, and it is thus hard to conclude that a tourism boycott for economic purposes would now suddenly change the government's attitude.

Amnesty International is a major human rights campaign NGO that has increasingly focused on tourism related rights violations in Israeli occupied Palestine. In response to the maintenance, development, and expansion of settlements that have been condemned as illegal in many UN Security Council and other UN resolutions, Amnesty International criticized travel companies and called for an international boycott of Israeli tourism operating in the occupied Palestinian territories (Middle East Monitor (MEM), 2019). Amnesty criticized digital tourism platforms such as Airbnb, Booking.com, Expedia, and TripAdvisor for profiting from 'war crimes' by offering services to Israel's illegal settlements (MEM, 2019). In its report *Destination Occupation 2019*, Amnesty International accused these companies for 'contributing to violations of human rights law and acting in direct contradiction with their own corporate standards' through their promotion of Israeli settlements in the occupied Palestinian territories. Their support for Israeli tourism was also criticised for 'normalizing, and legitimizing to the public what is recognized under international law as an illegal situation' (Amnesty International, 2019). Amnesty's report is part of its global campaign – launched in 2017 – which calls on governments to prevent businesses based in their countries from operating in Israeli settlements. While companies profiting from the illegal settlement enterprise have long been the subject of campaigns by human rights group, the widening of these protests to include digital travel companies is a new development that reflects the growing role of such platforms in the economics of tourism (MEM, 2019). Tourism activities are also significant as economic use can be a justification for territorial claims under international law (Hall, 1994a, 2008).

Not surprisingly, Israel rejected Amnesty's International call to boycott Israeli touristic sites in the West Bank (what Israel refers to Judea and Samaria). Israeli Strategic Affairs and Public Security Minister Gilad Erdan tweeted that 'Amnesty has become a leader in the anti-Semitic BDS campaign, and tonight's report on Israel is an outrageous attempt to distort the facts, deny Jewish heritage and delegitimize Israel' (quoted in Lempkowicz, 2019). Israeli Minister of Tourism Yariv Levin stated:

No force in the world will change the simple historical truth – the Land of Israel belongs to the People of Israel. . . . we will fight this despicable anti-Semitic decision, and we will not allow anyone to boycott Israel or parts of it . . . tourism to Israel and to Judea and Samaria is at an all-time height, and this is the best answer to shameful decisions of this kind.

(quoted in Lempkowicz, 2019)

In response to Amnesty's boycott call, Airbnb initially delisted 200 properties in November 2018 and ceased its operations in Israeli settlements in the occupied West Bank. Israel strongly denounced Airbnb's decision and threatened legal action against the company while it was welcomed by Palestinian officials and the international community, with Airbnb reversing its initial decision on delisting illegal Israeli settlements (MEM, 2019). One reason for the reversal was that Florida and other states were pressuring the company by examining whether Airbnb breached their state laws prohibiting them from doing business with entities that boycott Israel. In essence Airbnb found themselves caught between supporting a human rights action in the West Bank and legal sanctions in the US to stop such actions – in the end economic as opposed to human rights arguments one.

A similar case of competing sanctions and boycotts was experienced in 2017 when President Trump's executive order banning travel to the USA from seven predominantly Muslim countries, Iran, Iraq, Libya, Somalia, Sudan, Syria, and Yemen, for 90 days was followed by citizens from various countries around the world boycotting the United States as a travel destination. These controversial travel bans and restrictive measures of mobility and the accompanying perceptions and confusion the measures created in third countries resulted in a swift drop in the number of tourists to the United States and illustrated that the imposition of sanctions not only affects targeted countries but also perceptions of ease of traveller access (Taylor, 2017). Since the introduction of the first travel ban in January 2017 to October 2017, there was a 1.4% decline in international visitors as compared to the same period the previous year, which translated into substantial losses for the US economy (Taylor, 2017). This issue was also subject to significant domestic debate as the restrictions not only affect inbound tourists but also students, business travellers and workers, refugees, family members, and diasporic communities in the US, and thousands faced indefinite separation from family members from affected countries (Morello & Reardon, 2017; Reardon, 2017).

Animals' welfare concerns and boycott of tourism destination

The high number of boycotts related to animal welfare concerns reflects growing public concern about the welfare of animals. A study by the Humane Research Council (2008) in America found that calling for a boycott was one action that was supported by the public to end animal cruelty, a sentiment that parallels the findings of Shaheer et al. (2019). Richards (2019) argues that: 'Boycotts have been very effective at reducing cruelty to animals and improving animal welfare, and historically boycotts have been extremely effective in bringing about progressive social change'.

Organizations, such as Ethical Consumer, People for the Ethical Treatment of Animals (PETA), Companion Animal Protection Society (CAPS), Humane Farming Association's (HFA), and Buycott, are very active in in organizing animal rights boycotts by listing the companies, countries, destination, or businesses on their boycott list on their website for their inhumane treatment of animals. Tourist attractions that have animals as part of their tourist product, such as performing and/or captive display animals, are increasingly coming under pressure from animal rights activism while the hospitality sector is also having to respond to animal concern in its meal servings and its supply chain. Examples include calls to boycott foie gras because of arguments that force-feeding geese and ducks constitutes animal cruelty (Gille, 2011). The HFA's National Veal Boycott in the US reduced veal production from a high of 3.4 million calves to less than 600,000. Peta's campaign against KFC sought to encourage consumers to boycott KFC for supporting cruelty to chickens as a result of battery farming while asking KFC to adopt an animal welfare program with specific recommendations.

In many cases, public outcry over the abuse of animals has been so strong that boycotts of the tourism industry have been organized. In Kerala, India, the inhumane killing of dogs, turtles, and rabbits prompted the creation of a petition with the aim of appealing to international visitors to stay away from Kerala (Fennell, 2012; Care 2, 2019). In a situation similar to campaigns against bullfighting in Spain, Irish groups launched a Europe-wide campaign to boycott tourism in India because of the contact game of Jallikattu which involves hundreds of men surrounding a bull for the purpose of hitting it and wrestling the animal to the ground. The animals are made to drink alcohol and have chilli powder rubbed in their eyes before the 'game' commences (Suroor, 2012, cited in Fennell, 2012). In a broader context the NGO Friends of Animals (2006) called for a boycott of the Alaskan tourism industry in response to the government's wolf population control policies. Travel companies and destinations are often very sensitive over animal rights issues in Western visitor markets (Zapata Campos et al., 2018). Such issues clearly highlight different cultural values and perceptions as well as ethics with respect to animals and the environment. In some cases the importance of meeting market perceptions may be crucial for preventing consumer boycotts. However, in others the overall impact of consumer concern may not be sufficient to outweigh other motivations to visit a destination (Box 3.6).

Political boycott and tourism

Jews and Arabs have been boycotting one another since the early days of Zionism. In the decades before Israel's founding, the mainstream Zionist movement waged campaigns to boycott Arab workers, reject Arab produce, exclude Arabs from Jewish-only residential communities and forbid Arab purchase of Jewish-owned land. The fifth Palestine Arab Congress called for a boycott of Jewish goods in 1922. After Israel occupied the West Bank and Gaza in 1967, Palestinian lawyers boycotted Israeli courts, and teachers went on strike under the slogan, "no education under occupation". Israel responded to these and other acts of civil disobedience with arrests, fines, travel restrictions, shop closures, curfews and deportations of teachers, lawyers, mayors and university presidents.

(Thrall, 2018)

Box 3.6 Can the hunting and tourist consumption of a species co-exist in the same destination? The case of Iceland

Nature-tourism and the natural environment are the main reason for tourist visitation to Iceland (Sæþórsdóttir & Hall, 2019; Sæþórsdóttir, Hall, & Stefánsson, 2019). Whale-watching tourism is a significant marine tourism activity in Iceland, although Iceland still allows commercial whale harvesting with whale meat often being a feature of tourist menus. However, these activities are often considered to be incompatible in the tourist market, and it has been suggested that whale-watch tourists would boycott whale-watch destinations where whaling takes place, although evidence for this occurring is limited (Parsons & Rawles, 2003; Bertulli, Leeney, Barreau, & Matassa, 2016; Singleton, 2018). Bertulli et al. (2016) assessed the perceptions of and attitudes towards ongoing whaling amongst whale-watch tourists in Iceland and found that a majority of whale-watching tourists in did not support whaling and did not think that whale-watching and whaling could co-exist. Almost a third of their respondents were unaware that whaling was occurring in Iceland before their visit although most of these indicated that prior knowledge of whaling activities would not have affected their choice of Iceland as a destination. These results clearly suggest that the continuing tradition of whaling in Iceland does not override the overall attractiveness of the Icelandic environment to tourists with only limited likelihood of any travel boycott affecting visitor arrivals, with factors such as cost and more general perceptions of the environment being far more significant.

Box 3.7 What are boycotts, divestment and sanctions?

BOYCOTTS involve withdrawing support from Israel's apartheid regime, complicit Israeli sporting, cultural and academic institutions, and from all Israeli and international companies engaged in violations of Palestinian human rights.

DIVESTMENT campaigns urge banks, local councils, churches, pension funds, and universities to withdraw investments from the State of Israel and all Israeli and international companies that sustain Israeli apartheid.

SANCTIONS campaigns pressure governments to fulfil their legal obligations to end Israeli apartheid and not aid or assist its maintenance by banning business with illegal Israeli settlements, ending military trade and free-trade agreements, as well as suspending Israel's membership in international forums such as UN bodies and FIFA.

Source: BDS (2019)

Politics are a significant factor in boycotts and, as we have seen, in sanctions. Indeed, arguably all boycotts are political as they involve power relationships and attempts to change them. However, politics in the context of tourism boycotts has usually been connected to issues of regime change, state authority, and territorial disputes. Consumers, activists, and tourists have long responded to political conflict and issues in the form of boycott which has become a popular tool to express dissatisfaction towards perceived unacceptable behavior or policies of states and associated agencies, businesses, and individuals.

Perhaps one of the most prominent and longstanding political boycotts is the Palestinian-led Boycott, Divestment and Sanctions (BDS) movement (Box 3.7). The BDS was stablished in 2005 by Palestinian civil society organizations as a means to exert non-violent pressure on Israel in order to object to Israeli policies in general – and its economy and military in particular – in relation to occupied Palestine (Thrall, 2018). Inspired by the South African anti-apartheid movement, the Palestinian BDS urges nonviolent pressure on Israel until it complies with international law by meeting three demands (bdsmovement.net):

1   ending its occupation and colonization of all Arab lands and dismantling the Wall,

2   recognizing the fundamental rights of the Arab-Palestinian citizens of Israel to full equality, and
3   respecting, protecting, and promoting the rights of Palestinian refugees to return to their homes and properties as stipulated in UN Resolution 194.

The BDS movement seeks to boycott Israeli sporting, cultural, and academic institutions and ban investment in and trade with Israeli-based companies or organizations. 'BDS does not call for a boycott of individuals because she or he happens to be Israeli or because they express certain views', and they condemn 'all forms of racism, including Islamophobia and anti-Semitism' (Palestinian BDS National Committee quoted in Fischer, 2019).

The BDS movement is complementary to – but more international than – the boycott put in place by the Arab League in December 1945, shortly after its formation, before the establishment of the State of Israel in 1948 (see Box 3.1). The Arab League boycott, which is more akin to formal sanctions along with specific policy settings, is an effort by its member states to isolate Israel economically to prevent Arab states and discourage non-Arabs from providing support to Israel and adding to Israel's economic and military strength. In tourism terms the scope of this boycott has led to severed road and rail links with neighboring Arab countries, the prohibition of direct air flights from Arab League countries, preventing overflights over Arab airspace by Israeli aircraft, and the refusal of third country airlines that fly into Israel. Originally, the Arab boycott had a moderate negative impact on Israel's economy and development. Inevitably the economies of participating Arab nations also suffered as the result of a deterioration in the foreign direct investment climate in the Arab world and reduction in the volume of trade. The Organization of Islamic Cooperation (OIC) has also urged its members to join in the Arab League boycott of Israel in the form of diplomatic boycott, again reflecting the sanctions dimension. The call was renewed on 22 May 2018, when the OIC recommended to its 57 members a selective ban on some Israeli goods because of the events in Gaza and the opening of the United States embassy in Jerusalem. As a result of boycotts and sanctions, Israeli passports are not recognized and accepted by 16 Arab and OIC countries including Algeria, Bangladesh, Brunei, Iran, Iraq, Kuwait, Lebanon, Libya, Malaysia, Oman, Pakistan, Saudi Arabia, Sudan, Syria, United Arab Emirates, and Yemen. Eight of these also do not accept passports of other countries whose holder has an Israeli visa endorsed in it.

On a purely geographic basis, Israel should be a member of the Asia-Pacific UN Group but Arab and Muslim nations have blocked Israel from joining. As a result Israel was blocked from the regional group system for 39 years, and only in December 2013 was Israel granted full membership of the Western European and Others Group (WEOG) in Geneva, entitling Israel to participate in Geneva-based UN bodies, such as the UN Human Rights Council.

Israel has been exposed to a sports boycott by Arab countries and Israel's flag and anthem are often excluded at international sporting events in Arab countries. More controversially, Israeli sport teams have sometimes been denied visas to compete in competitions. For example, Israeli chess players were not granted visas for an international chess tournament in Saudi Arabia as the country does not have official diplomatic relations with Israel. In July 2018, the World Chess Federation said it would forbid Tunisia from hosting international chess competitions if they refused a visa to Israel's champion (Schreiber, 2018). In addition, sporting teams from various Arab states and especially Iran continue to boycott Israeli athletes at international matches. When they are drawn against an Israeli team, some teams and individuals sometimes choose instead to forfeit the match. Indeed, when in 2019 an Iranian judo athlete, Saeid Mollaei, was pressurised by Iranian authorities to drop out before his quarter-final at the world judo championships in Tokyo to avoid the prospect of fighting Israel's Sagi Muki in the final and refused, he said he could seek asylum in Germany because of concerns for his family and himself.

Under the BDS campaign the extent of boycott has widened to include academic and cultural boycotts as well as the economic and spatial focus. Importantly – and arguably underappreciated by many – the scope of the campaign also means that actions of other governments in the region are as much under scrutiny for their positions on Palestine as is the Israeli government. The BDS campaign therefore seeks to be non-violent and comprehensive in its approach.

The initial campaign for an academic boycott of Israel was first launched in April 2004 by a group of Palestinian academics and intellectuals in Ramallah, in the West Bank, as a part of the BDS movement, which led to the formation of the Palestinian Campaign for the Academic and Cultural Boycott of Israel (PACBI). This campaign aims to exert severe international pressure on Israeli academic institutions. Since then, proposals for academic boycotts of particular Israeli universities and academics have been made by academics and organizations in the Palestinian territories, the United States (the endorsement of a boycott of Israeli academic institutions by American Studies Association (ASA) in 2013); the United Kingdom (e.g. the National Association of Teachers in Further and Higher Education and the Association of University Teachers (AUT) in 2006); and other countries (e.g. Spanish organizers of an international solar power design competition excluded a team from the Israeli Ariel University Center in 2009; suspension of ties with Israeli Ben-Gurion University by the University of Johannesburg in

2011; boycotting Israel's Institute of Technology, Technion by 168 Italian academics and researchers in January 2016). Perhaps the most public aspect of the academic boycott of Israel was the decision by Stephen Hawking not to participate in the Jerusalem-based Israeli Presidential Conference hosted by Israeli president Shimon Peres in 2013. A statement published by the British Committee for the Universities of Palestine with Hawking's approval described it as 'his independent decision to respect the boycott, based upon his knowledge of Palestine, and on the unanimous advice of his own academic contacts there' (Sherwood & Kalman, 2013). Hawking had visited Israel four times previously. However, in 2009 Hawking denounced Israel's three-week attack on Gaza, telling Al-Jazeera that Israel's response to rocket fire from Gaza was 'plain out of proportion. . . . The situation is like that of South Africa before 1990 and cannot continue' (quoted in Sherwood & Kalman, 2013). Israel Maimon, chairman of the presidential conference said:

> This decision is outrageous and wrong. The use of an academic boycott against Israel is outrageous and improper, particularly for those to whom the spirit of liberty is the basis of the human and academic mission. Israel is a democracy in which everyone can express their opinion, whatever it may be. A boycott decision is incompatible with open democratic discourse.
>
> (quoted in Sherwood & Kalman, 2013)

A number of strategies have been used to counter the BDS movement. Israel passed legislation in 2011 that makes support of the boycott by an individual or organization illegal and provides a basis for both refusing entry into the country as well as seeking to apply extra-territorial law. Under the law calling for a boycott is a civil offense that can result in compensation being liable to be paid regardless of the actual damage caused. The legislation defines a boycott as 'deliberately avoiding economic, cultural or academic ties with another person or another factor only because of his ties with the State of Israel, one of its institutions or an area under its control, in such a way that may cause economic, cultural or academic damage' (Sherwood & Kalman, 2013). Yossi Kuperwasser led the Israeli government's efforts against the BDS movement until 2014. According to Kuperwasser

> The core issue is not whether they are going to boycott us or not boycott us. . . . The core issue is whether [the BDS . . . movement is] going to be successful in implanting in the international discourse that Israel is illegitimate as a Jewish state. . . . If you want to promote the boycotting

of Israel, any part of Israel, you are not a friend of Israel. You are actually an enemy of Israel. So we have to deal with you.

(quoted in Thrall, 2018)

Israel has therefore been actively campaigning internationally against the BDS movement (Box 3.8). Cohen and Avraham (2018) conducted an analysis of seven North American Jewish NGOs and their strategies against the BDS that reflect the broader Israeli approach to the boycott campaign. They identified three main strategies:

1   source strategies – which present the BDS movement and its promoters as anti-Semitic and questions their goals and claims that the movement is based on a desire to destroy Israel;
2   message strategies – which aim to present contrary information to BDS claims regarding Israel (such as it being an apartheid state) and promote a more positive image of Israel; and
3   specific target audience strategies – present Israel as a democratic country in a non-democratic region to Western audiences and suggest to Western audiences that they share the same values as Israel.

Another form of political boycott is the use of boycott by religious groups. The role of religion and the religious value systems in shaping consumer

---

Box 3.8   German parliament declares BDS boycott campaign antisemitic

In May 2019, Germany's Bundestag has become the first parliament in Europe to pass a motion labelling the BDS movement against Israel as antisemitic. The non-binding motion, said the campaign to boycott Israeli artists and goods, was 'reminiscent of the most terrible chapter in German history' and triggered memories of the Nazis' slogan: 'Don't buy from Jews' (Oltermann, 2019). In response, an open letter signed by 60 Jewish and Israeli academics criticized the motion, saying it formed part of an alarming trend of 'labelling supporters of Palestinian human rights as antisemitic'. The open letter said that the conflation of BDS and antisemitism was supported by 'Israel's most right-wing government in history' and formed part of a strategy to delegitimize any attempt at international solidarity with the Palestinian cause (Oltermann, 2019).

Source: Oltermann (2019)

behavior has been recognized by different studies (Essoo & Dibb, 2004; Al-Hyari, Alnsour, Al-Weshah, & Haffar, 2012). According to Al-Hyari et al. (2012), the purchasing behavior and consumption practices are not only restricted by social, political, and economic opportunities but also influenced by the cultural frameworks of consumers' environments and their religious value system (Al-Hyari et al., 2012). Notable examples include Christian fundamentalists boycott of *Jerry Springer the Opera* when it was staged in the UK due to the portrayal of Jesus as a homosexual (Thomas, 2010) and the campaigns against Monty Python's film *Life of Brian*, often by people who had never seen it and who also did not understand the film's grounding in the scriptures and biblical scholarship (Davies, 2004; Crossley, 2011). The banning the wearing of religious symbols – or what are perceived as religious symbols – by certain organizations and countries has recently been subjected to debate and in some cases resulted in expressions of dissatisfaction by consumers (Crumley, 2004). Literature can also be a point of contention with book burning often being a form of protest or political statement. In 2007, in reaction to the writer Salman Rushdie having received an award for his work from the British Government, there were demands to boycott British embassies and goods in the Arab and Muslim world by those who believe that Rushdie offended the symbols of Islam, the prophet Mohamed, and the holy Quran (Hoyle, 2007). Iran also boycotted the Frankfurt book fair in 2015 because organizers had invited Salman Rushdie to deliver the keynote address at the opening press conference (Dehghan, 2015).

Consumers in Muslim and Middle Eastern countries were urged to boycott Danish goods as a result of a religious conflict following the publication of Prophet Mohammed caricatures in a Danish newspaper (Knight, Mitchell, & Gao, 2009). Ayman al-Zawahiri of Al-Qaeda urged all Muslims to boycott not only Denmark but also Norway, France, Germany, and all others that had 'insulted the Prophet Mohammed' by printing cartoons depicting him (New Zealand was also included at one time but this was generally believed to be a geographical mistake by Al-Qaeda as they confused New Zealand with the Dutch Zeeland region). Consumer goods companies were the most vulnerable to the boycott; among companies heavily affected were Arla Foods, Novo Nordisk, and Danisco. Arla, Denmark's biggest exporter to the Middle East, lost ten million kroner (1.6 million US dollars, 1.3 million euros) per day in the initial weeks of the boycott (Allagui, 2006). The Muslim boycott of Danish goods was estimated to cost Danish businesses around 134 million euros overall and was attributed as the cause of an approximate 50% decline in exports to the Middle East (BBC, 2006). Scandinavian tourism to Egypt also fell by between 20% and 30% in the first two months of 2006 (www.politiken.dk, 2006).

Nevertheless, Farah and Newman (2010) argue that it is the political inclinations of consumers rather than their religious orientations that affect their decisions to participate in boycott campaigns. They explain this as follows:

> This is especially the case when boycott campaigns are promoted by the Arab Nationalist and Lebanese Communist Parties known for their historical contempt for American foreign policies. Since the creation of the Republic in 1943 the Lebanese have disagreed over the identity of the state. Muslims are inclined towards a close association with Greater Syria and the Arab World; whereas Christians, particularly the Maronites, opt to link Lebanon culturally and politically to the Western World. This division in identity and beliefs within the Lebanese society affects the composition of groups participating in the boycott as a support for the Arab cause and a sign of rejection of American interventions.
>
> (Farah & Newman, 2010, p. 353)

Environmental boycott and tourism

Growing concerns over perceived threats to environmental quality, climate change, biodiversity loss, and unsustainable environmental practices have prompted the creation of environmental pressure groups to protest the offending actions of corporations and governments (Carter, 2018). Since the creation of the first environmental activist organization, the Sierra Club, at the turn of the twentieth century, such groups have become significant players in pro-conservation protest actions and are significant political actors given the importance of the environment to many voters. Examples of such organizations include Extinction Rebellion, Friends of the Earth, Greenpeace, Earth Island Institute, People for the Ethical Treatment of Animals (PETA), Earth First!, Sea Shepherd, the Australian Conservation Foundation, The Wilderness Society, and the Rainforest Action Network. The growing number of environmental organizations along with the growth of ecologically conscious consumers has run parallel with the growth of environmentally oriented boycotts on countries, regions, agencies, businesses, and corporations.

Environmental or ecological boycotts occur when consumers perceive that a company or state is acting in a harmful or abusive way towards the environment. Perhaps surprisingly, given how widespread such boycotts are, many studies related to boycotting (Abosag & Farah, 2014; Sen et al., 2001; Friedman, 1999) have overlooked the importance of ecological boycotts (Nguyen et al., 2018). There are also limited studies on the motivation to participate in ecological boycotts given the increasing consumers' participation in the boycott by the increase of environmentally sensitive consumers (Cho & Krasser, 2011; García-de-Frutos, Ortega-Egea, & Martínez-del-Río, 2018). As ecologically conscious consumers emerged in the 1960s in light of growing concerns over pollution and the environment (Kinnear, Taylor, & Ahmed, 1974) boycotts and buycotts have come to be increasingly used as a means to encourage the greening of industries, corporations, and government policies (Leonidou, Leonidou, & Kvasova, 2010; Delacote, 2009). These have met with a degree of success, however, there are also concerns over the extent to which destinations, businesses, attractions, and events engage in greenwashing in an attempt to placate consumers (Hall, 2012; Gaffney, 2013; Miller, 2016).

Consumer boycotts are a common strategy used by many environmental NGOs that have both direct and indirect impacts on tourism and hospitality. Examples include:

- the boycott of cosmetic firms, e.g. Procter and Gamble, Colgate-Palmolive, for their use of animal testing (Davidson, 1995) – such boycotts and impacts on the perceived green qualities of brands have implications for hotel purchasing of soap and toiletries;
- the boycott of major oil companies, e.g. Total, ESSO, Shell, for the environmental damage caused by their products and their development and their lobbying efforts to deter climate change policies (Skjærseth & Skodvin, 2001) – has implications for consumer purchasing when engaged in holiday trips;
- the boycott of some large fast-food companies (e.g. McDonald's, KFC) for their supposed environmental unfriendly way to produce meat (Garret, 1987) – direct impact on restaurant sector and greater awareness in the hospitality industry on supply chain;
- the boycott of non-certified tropical timber by some NGOs to protest against unsustainable harvest practices and corruption (Klooster, 2005). In 2004, WALHI – Indonesia's largest environmental group – and several other environmental groups have called for a boycott of timber from Indonesia, Malaysia, Singapore, and China, countries where illegal logging plagues local development and environmental indicators – has implications for the use of sustainable timber products in tourism and hospitality, especially for businesses that seek to position themselves as green. There are also potential effects on destination brands as a result of unsustainable environmental practices, such as forest clearfelling and burning; and
- the call by environmental and animal rights activists to boycott the US state of Iowa as a vacation destination in 2019 given that the state governor signed off legislation to support controversial 'ag-gag' laws, just

months after a federal court declared them unconstitutional (McCormick, 2019). The legislation, which will make it illegal to use 'deception' to gain access to an agricultural facility are a response to activist efforts to document conditions, e.g. by camera phone, inside industrial agricultural facilities

Summary and conclusions

This chapter has highlighted the implications of consumer boycott, the individual or collective choice of not buying some product, along with other forms of political consumerism (McLaughlin, 2004), such as buycotts, on tourism and hospitality (Box 3.9). As with sanctions, boycotts can have both direct and indirect implications for tourism. Such a situation is significant as boycotts appear to be an increasingly used tool of NGOs, lobby groups, consumer activists, and individual citizens to protest against perceived unfair marketing and social, political, and environmental practices. Indeed, these consumption practices constitute a way to signal positive and negative preferences and to reconcile consumption with social, environmental, and political, human rights and/or health considerations.

Consumer boycotts may also be interpreted as a way for unsatisfied consumers to compensate for government policy or inactivity in relation to rights and justice issues. This has arguably become increasingly significant because of the impact of deregulation and market-oriented governance strategies. In such situations, boycotts and buycotts could be regarded as constituting a substitute for public policies and formal sanctions regimes. The objective of boycotts is to put enough pressure on the target to change and adopt fair policies and practices that meet certain international or societal norms. This was the case in apartheid South Africa, and serves as an example for the BDS (2019) campaign against 'Israeli apartheid and settler-colonialism' policies (Thrall, 2018). Although, as these cases demonstrate, such boycotts can be highly contested and divisive, with consumer and NGO action often running ahead of government and business. Consumer and NGO boycott demands on business and government may also prove to be contentious, although as this chapter has noted about a quarter of such campaigns appear to achieve their immediate goals, although the longer-term impacts on brand values and consumer perceptions remain unclear.

Tourism is intimately bound up in such processes and issues, being the direct and indirect subject of boycott activity. However, again, it is worth bearing in mind that some tourists will go to a destination or support a business in response to threats of a boycott. Nevertheless, while human rights and politics are an extremely significant part of boycotting activity, other concerns such as the environment – including animal rights – and work

Box 3.9 Political consumerism and online information and communication in boycotts and buycotts

Kelm and Dohle (2018) undertook two studies of German political consumers and their engagement in boycotts and buycotts together with their engagement in online communication. The found that that the frequency of political consumerism is influenced by the intensity of (online) information and (online) communication. Socio-demographics, political interest, and political orientation appear to be better factors than information and communication intensity for explaining whether people are political consumers or not. In contrast, information and communication intensities appear to be critical factors in determining how active political consumers are. Both offline (Shah et al., 2007) and online communication activities appear to mediate the influence of information frequency on political consumerism

Kelm and Dohle's (2018) results also suggest that boycotts are more influenced by communication activities than buycotts, which they believe is probably because boycotts are more of a collective activity that require greater organizational effort than buycotts. Given ease of information availability, the intensity of online information was found to have a larger impact on boycotts and buycotts compared to the intensity of offline information. However, overall they concluded

> Face-to-face communication is still more influential on political consumerism activities than communication via the Internet – maybe because in offline communication, greater social pressure can be exerted than in more anonymous online communication situations; another possibility is that individuals have more confidence in information provided in person (i.e. face to face) than in information transmitted online.
>
> (Kelm & Dohle, 2018, p. 1539)

Source: Kelm and Dohle (2018)

conditions are also growing in importance. These issues are potentially substantial drivers of boycotts and buycotts at the firm level, especially through the supply chain, although destinations may also be affected. Regardless, political consumerism is an important force in tourism and hospitality that requires greater recognition from government and business, as well as the research community.

4 Sanctions and boycotts as the new ethical tourism?

The future of sanctions and boycotts in an interconnected world

> Your choice of holiday destination is a political act. Tourism is also a way for governments to assert their ideologies – internally and externally. . . .Tourism is an industry tied up with national and international politics like no other. Tourists are a source of foreign exchange, governments promote themselves through visitors, and politicians quite often worry about the social freedom that tourism can nurture. For these reasons tourists are both courted and scapegoated.
>
> (Canavan, 2018)

This final chapter takes a brief look at some of the emerging and potential future issues with respect to sanctions and boycotts in a tourism context and reinforces the suggestion of Canavan (2018) that destination selection, access, and denial are inherently political acts. It revisits the popularity and success of sanctions and boycotts before addressing emerging research concerns. The chapter then addresses some of the issues that are likely to become the subject of sanctions and boycotts in the near future, such as anthropogenic climate change and biodiversity loss and the way in which they will likely impinge upon tourism.

Why are sanctions so popular?

> Economic sanctions have been integral to the repertoire of coercive foreign policy measures for centuries. Throughout this time, the imposition of sanctions has involved the dynamic interaction between the policies of implementation and maintenance, on the one hand, and various political and economic calculations of effectiveness on the other.
>
> (Cortright & Lopez, 2018b, p. 3)

Sanctions are playing a growing role in modern geopolitics and are used for a variety of reasons, from promoting human rights to impeding nuclear proliferation. They can target states, individuals, or businesses and take many forms, including travel bans, asset freezes, and trade embargoes. Tourism is rarely the direct subject of a sanction, although limits on the capacity of individuals to engage in outbound or inbound travel are clearly direct, as in the case of citizens of the US travelling to Cuba for example, the effects of country-wide sanctions, as in the cases of Cuba, Turkey, and Iran, are substantial (see Chapter 2). What is extremely significant for the tourism industry, whether as the target of sanctions or as the competing beneficiary, is that the use of sanctions appears to be growing. The UN Security Council has imposed sanctions more than 20 times since the end of the Cold War, typically in cases where diplomacy has failed and military options are unviable. The EU has levied sanctions more than 30 times, in addition to those mandated by the UN. The US, meanwhile, uses economic and financial sanctions more than any other country, which given the role of the US dollar in international trade and the extra-territorial nature of US sanctions law has global business and economic repercussions.

Arguably, the reluctance to get directly involved in foreign conflicts is a major factor in the growing popularity of sanctions. This also potentially points to another significant factor in their use in that while sanctions operate internationally, they may well be developed and actioned for a domestic audience to indicate that something is being done to deal with a specific issue. For example, in the US context domestic audiences and special interest groups can have a major role in foreign policy decision making in relation to sanctions (Kline, 1999; Fisk, 2000; Hufbauer & Oegg, 2003; Aridan, 2017), while the role of domestic political concerns has also been identified with respect to Japanese sanctions on North Korea (Hughes, 2006). Interestingly, Lektzian and Souva (2003) argued that democracies impose sanctions more often than other regime types because they encompass a greater variety of interest groups. Yet, institutional incentives for successful foreign policies lead democracies to prefer sanctioning non-democracies instead of democracies. Furthermore, democratic regimes are more likely than non-democracies to impose financial sanctions and pursue minor foreign policy goals. Kustra (2018) investigated whether the size of a diaspora's voting bloc in US swing states determined whether the American government imposed sanctions on their former homeland. In considering dictatorships from 1946 to 2005, Kustra (2018) found that a one-percentage-point increase in the size of a country's diaspora in swing states increased the probability of sanctions by 11%. McLean and Whang (2014) provide a more complex analysis of US sanctions and argue that senders design sanction policies in response to two domestic constituencies and argue that, after policymakers announce a sanctions policy, interest groups that stand to experience economic losses from the implementation of sanctions pressure policymakers to choose measures that limit their losses. As a result, they conclude that policymakers design sanction policies to include measures that are less detrimental to domestic special interest groups.

Allen (2008a, 2008b) also provides a more critical account of the importance of domestic politics in understanding the success of sanctions, though in her case it is focussed on the target state. As she notes, the domestic politics of the target state are significant causal mechanisms with respect to the success or failure of sanctions policies. Allen (2008b, p. 939) suggests 'Sanctioners often impose sanctions with the expectation (or perhaps simple hope) that sanctions will lead to increased political fragmentation within the target'. But, from her analysis of domestic political action expressed by protest and rebellion events in sanctioned states, she concludes that while 'it is apparent that sanctions can lead to an increase in mass political action, . . . that increase seems to be limited in autocratic states. Only in states with some degree of political openness and opportunity do sanctions increase the willingness of the public to take anti[-]government action' (Allen, 2008b, p. 939). This means that the political institutions of the target state are an important moderator of the influence of sanctions in encouraging domestic change from within targets. Where political freedoms are limited, as in the case of theocracies like Iran for example (see Chapter 2), sanctions do not encourage local opposition to take action against governing regimes. Allen (2008b, p. 939) therefore suggests

> If sanctions are not creating domestic political costs for autocratic leaders, it is imperative for sanctions senders to find ways to create external international costs for autocrats who refuse to comply with sanctions pressure. Without facing some political cost associated with sanctions, these leaders will have little or no incentive to alter their behavior. Freezing the personal assets of leaders, curtailing travel, and limiting exposure to the international community can focus the hardship of sanctions more directly on these leaders themselves. This may be necessary, as these results suggest that sanctions themselves will not lead to domestic costs in these states, at least not via political pressure from the general public.

As Chapter 2 noted, sanctions, at least with respect to changing the behavior or policies of target states, are not greatly successful (Morgan & Schwebach, 1997; Pape, 1997; Early, 2015; Haidar, 2017; Krain, 2017). However, their success may perhaps be more appropriately judged by the response of domestic interest groups and voters.

Several trends are likely to emerge with respect to the future evolution of international sanctions. First, the use of sanctions in the international relations landscape will potentially be affected by changes in the contemporary international order. This can be observed in the relative political and economic decline of traditionally sanctioning actors (i.e. the European Union and the United States) and the (re)emergence of actors such as China and Russia. The performance of sanctions depends to a large extent on the economic asymmetry between the sanctioning country and the sanctioned country. But given the contemporary globalization and the emergence of new powers, economic asymmetry has a tendency to be reduced among the major world powers. This includes the United States, which is the central actor involved with extraterritoriality issues of the international sanctions' regime along with the EU, which has been faced with the implications of the Brexit crisis as well as with the resurgence of nationalism, along with the United Nations. A second and related trend is the potential use of sanctions within a regional context by regional 'powers' within their sphere of influence; this may be especially significant in terms of the actions of countries such as Nigeria and South Africa in sub-Saharan Africa, Brazil in South America, or Australia in the Pacific. However, this is an area of relatively little research in a tourism context.

A third dimension, which also relates to the significance of domestic actors in the sender state, is that the use of the sanction may also be more a business logic than a real choice of foreign policy. From this context sanctions therefore need to be understood within the wider context of economic statecraft rather than as purely a political mechanism. Matelly, Gomez, and Carcanague (2017) argue that:

> The sanction can indeed be part of competition logic (weakening of a sector in the sanctioned country by targeting investments or technologies for example) or in a protectionist logic (national production revitalized by an embargo on imports, such as this is currently the case in Russia in the agricultural sector). This instrument of sanction may be a traditional political objective, but also a strategy closer to economic warfare than foreign policy as such, with the primary aim of supporting national economic interests. In the latter case, the risk is real for the international community since it would correspond to a mercantilist policy, which could be at the source of conflicts and instabilities. Moreover, they are policies that go against the multilateral and liberal choices made by the major international organizations.

The evolution of sanctions practices over time is also linked with the more general evolution of coercive policy in the contemporary world order. Given the ever-increasing reluctance of public opinion to support armed intervention as 'hard means', international sanctions have been multiplied as 'soft means', especially when it comes to cases where other options are limited as in the case of civil war in Syria. In the absence of clear policy alternatives, sanctions often constitute the core of international actors' response to such conflicts. As Masters (2019) explains:

> Governments and multinational bodies impose economic sanctions to try to alter the strategic decisions of state and non-state actors that threaten their interests or violate international norms of behavior. Critics say sanctions are often poorly conceived and rarely successful in changing a target's conduct, while supporters contend they have become more effective in recent years and remain an essential foreign policy tool. Sanctions have been the defining feature of the Western response to several geopolitical challenges, including North Korea's nuclear program and Russia's intervention in Ukraine. In recent years, the United States has expanded the use of sanctions, applying them and ramping them up against adversaries in Iran, Russia, Syria, and Venezuela.

The changing role of public opinion is altering the perception and use of sanctions. Mobilization of public opinion by state actors and the increasing role of NGOs can affect companies or states in the form of a consumer boycott or symbolic and mediatized actions. The latter shapes a new form of large-scale international sanction, going beyond the simple local or national boycott that existed prior to globalization. Reputational harm represents a real economic risk for companies, countries, and destinations, whether they act within the law or not (Box 4.1). They may then give up working with certain actors or in certain markets to avoid risk taking or damage to their image. The ever increasing speed of information flows reinforces the effects of such attacks. These phenomena, comparable to informal sanctions, could be multiplied by more active and connected civil societies and may well be relatively more successful in achieving their goals.

Research concerns and policy needs

Economic sanctions play the sometimes contradictory roles of multilateral peace-builder and foreign policy panacea (Cortright & Lopez, 2018b). Acknowledging this, Cortright and Lopez (2018b, p. 201) argue that:

> This duality results in part from the difficulty of applying an instrument that may not be fully understood to the varied and complex economic, military, and political dynamics of a contemporary world which itself defies full comprehension . . . our knowledge of the imposition, maintenance, effectiveness, and context of sanctions use lags far behind the needs of policymakers.

Box 4.1 Cathay Pacific and protest in Hong Kong

Mass protests began in Hong Kong on 9 June 2018, against a legislative bill that would have allowed for residents to stand trial in mainland China. Many protesters felt this bill would infringe on the city's autonomy, promised until 2047, under the 'one country, two systems' agreement with Beijing. Cathay Pacific, which is based in Hong Kong, initially supported the right of its staff to protest, its chairman saying that 'we certainly wouldn't dream of telling [our staff] what they have to think about something'. However, China's aviation authority told the airline that it would have to remove any staff involved in or supportive of protests from flights over its airspace, and almost all of Cathay's flights pass through Chinese airspace, while mainland Chinese customers and firms started to withdraw business. The chair of the flight attendants union at the Cathay Pacific subsidiary Cathay Dragon, Rebecca Sy, said she had been sacked after managers presented her with copies of protest-related Facebook posts. Cathay Pacific, which said that the measure was not related to her union activities, reiterated before the rally that it upheld Hong Kong's rights and freedoms but had a zero-tolerance approach 'to any support for or participation in illegal protests, violent activities or overly radical behavior'. In response hundreds of demonstrators gathered in Hong Kong to denounce Cathay Pacific for firing staff. According to one demonstrator, a retiree who gave her name as Miss Chan. 'It's not just an issue for Cathay . . . They want to [persuade] the public that if you go on a demonstration you may be punished; even if you are not arrested, you might lose employment opportunities. They are trying to expand the fear, which is already huge in Hong Kong'.

Source: Branigan and Hale (2019)

They also highlight the necessity of forming a research agenda with respect to the positioning of sanctions in contemporary foreign policy and suggest three areas for further research, all of which are germane to a better understanding of the relationships between tourism and sanctions: understanding the policy context of sanctions, assessing methods for improving the impact of sanctions, and investigating incentives as a means of persuasion.

Overall, the effectiveness of sanctions is largely influenced by the type of policy change pursued. Although sanctions are often justified as a means to protect human rights (see Chapter 2), research by Krain (2017) on genocides and politicides from 1976 to 2008 found that sanctions neither aggravate nor alleviate atrocities either on their own or combined with other policy options. These findings held regardless of whether they are measured as the number or presence of sanctions, their cost, comprehensiveness, duration, or whether imposed or administered by an international organization (Krain, 2017).

Perhaps one of the notable examples is the failure of US sanctions regime in the form of trade and travel embargo on Cuba, which is one of the longstanding sanctions regimes in history and, interestingly, achieved none of Washington's policy objectives (Early, 2015; Jeong & Peksen, 2019). After the fall of the Soviet Union, for example, Cuba improved its economic relations with third-party states, including with respect to tourism. For instance, foreign investment from Canada grew in Cuba's tourism and mining industries, while Canada lowered its overall tariff rates for Cuban imports in the latter half of the 1990s thereby increasing Cuba's exports to Canada. The amount of bilateral export and import flows, as well as having a significant tourism component between Cuba, the Netherlands, and Spain, increased for many of the same reasons (Barbieri, Keshk, & Pollins 2009; Early, 2015). Moreover, it is also argued that the longer sanctions last, the less likely they are to succeed. Rowat (2014) explains that:

> This reflects a fatigue in the countries imposing them as well as the target's growing experience evading the sanctions. In the case of Iraq in the 1990s, not only did the government become more adept at smuggling, but Iraq's neighbours grew tired of paying a price to enforce what they saw as a US policy whose burden within Iraq was primarily borne by the most vulnerable.

This is not to suggest that sanctions are without effect; they make trade more difficult and they do have economic impacts that can affect the general population. In the case of non-oil exports from Iran, for example, Haidar (2017) found that two-thirds of these exports were deflected to non-sanctioning countries after sanctions were imposed in 2008 and that aggregate exports actually increased following price reductions. Or it can be observed within the case of North Korea; the country has managed to sidestep UN sanctions for more than a decade. Perlez, Huang, and Mozur (2017) explain that:

> Despite seven rounds of United Nations sanctions over the past 11 years, including a ban on "bulk cash" transfers, large avenues of trade remain open to North Korea, allowing it to earn foreign currency to sustain its economy and finance its program to build a nuclear weapon that can strike the United States.

Trenin (2015) also argues that sanctions are most effective against friends and allies and less effective when applied to international foes – such as the restrictions imposed on Russia by Western powers – and can have unintended consequences. He further explains that:

> Politically, sanctions; in the case of adversaries, they can stiffen their resolve – at least in the short term. The sanctions imposed on Russia in 2014 during the crisis over Ukraine have contributed not just to a surge in Vladimir Putin's popularity but, more importantly, to the growth of Russian patriotism and nationalism. In moments of bravado, the Kremlin even hopes that a long period of sanctions can guarantee political stability in the country for many years.

Although it may strike the reader as strange that sanctions may be undertaken against international allies, it should be noted that such a move has been a part of US foreign policy strategies, particularly in terms of disagreeing with multilateral agreements and the international legal framework, if they do not meet with perceived US interests or the political goals of the Presidential incumbent (Box 4.2).

Box 4.2 Sanctions on sanctions: the US rejection of the International Court of Justice and the International Criminal Court

The US has long sought to withdraw itself from International Court of Justice (ICJ) jurisdiction. The IJC is the 'principal judicial organ' of the UN. Under Article 93 of the Charter, which the US ratified in 1945, all member nations of the UN also are parties to the ICJ Statute (Mulligan, 2018). The jurisdiction of the Court in contentious proceedings is based on the consent of the states to which it is open. In October 2018 the US announced that it was withdrawing from an ICJ protocol and pulled out of a 1955 friendship treaty with Iran after the ICJ ruled that US sanctions on Iran had to allow exemptions for exports of humanitarian and civil aviation supplies. The decision was binding but is unable to be enforced. As a result of the ruling along with a complaint brought to the ICJ by Palestine against the Trump administration's decision to move the US embassy in Israel from Tel Aviv to Jerusalem, the National Security Advisor, John Bolton, announced that the US would abandon the 'optional protocol'; under the *Vienna Convention on Diplomatic Relations*, a 1961 international treaty that frames the diplomatic relations between states. The decision to with-draw will limit US exposure to ICJ rulings, which will simultaneously restrict its own ability to bring cases against other countries. Accord-ing to Bolton, 'This really has less to do with Iran and the Palestinians than with the continued consistent policy of the United States to reject the jurisdiction of the International Court of Justice, which we think is politicized and ineffective' (quoted in Turak, 2018). The ICJ has subsequently ruled that Iran has the right to recover two billion dollars in frozen assets in the US which the US has argued must go to victims of attacks blamed on Iran. Although the US is no longer subject to the ICJ's broad compulsory jurisdiction, the US is a party to more than 80 international agreements with ICJ clauses (Mulligan, 2018).

A related international legal entity is the International Criminal Court (ICC). Although legally independent from the UN, the United Nations Security Council retains certain functional powers. The ICC has juris-diction to prosecute individuals for the international crimes of genocide, crimes against humanity, war crimes, and crimes of aggression. How-ever, its activities often face substantial opposition. In May 2002, the US withdrew its acceptance of the Rome statute, under which the ICC had been created, threatening to release, by military force if necessary, any indicted US citizens being held by the Court. Although Human Rights Watch and others condemned the US actions in August 2002, the US threatened to withdraw aid from countries that refused to recognise the immunity of US military personnel from ICC prosecution as well as restrict US participation in UN peacekeeping unless the US has immu-nity from prosecution (Shah, 2005). On 3 August 2002, US President George Bush signed into law the *American Servicemembers Protection Act (ASPA) of 2002* to give effect to these measures, although these provisions can be waived by the president on national interest grounds. In January 2019 Judge Christoph Flügge resigned from the ICC citing 'shocking' political interference. According to Flugge

> John Bolton, the national security adviser to the US president, held a speech last September in which he wished death on the international criminal court. . . . If these judges ever interfere in the domestic concerns of the US or investigate an American citizen, he said the American government would do all it could to ensure that these judges would no longer be allowed to travel to the United States – and that they would perhaps even be criminally prosecuted. . . . The American security adviser held his speech at a time when The Hague was planning preliminary

investigations into American soldiers who had been accused of torturing people in Afghanistan. The American threats against international judges clearly show the new political climate. It is shocking. I had never heard such a threat. . . . It is consistent with the new American line: 'We are No 1 and we stand above the law.'

(quoted in Boffey, 2019)

In March 2019 The US secretary of state Mike Pompeo announced that the US will revoke or deny visas to members of the ICC involved in investigating the actions of US troops in Afghanistan or other countries and that the country was prepared to take further steps, including economic sanctions on the ICC (AFP, 2019). In April judges at the ICC rejected a request by the court's top prosecutor to open an investigation into war crimes and crimes against humanity in Afghanistan, saying that any investigation and prosecution was unlikely to be successful because those targeted, including the US, Afghan authorities, and the Taliban, would not cooperate (Bowcott, 2019).

See: International Court of Justice: www.icj-cij.org/en; International Criminal Court: www.icc-cpi.int

Overall therefore, while often having an impact on tourism in the countries they are applied to, either directly by preventing foreign investment or restricting market access or indirectly by their effect on destination image, the capacity of sanctions to induce change in target states appears limited. Nevertheless, it is clear that they will be a continuing feature of coercive foreign policy well into the future, with their success often best evaluated in terms of domestic support of the sender rather than change in the target state. As a result, the domestic perceptions of sanctions in the sender and its long-term implications for perception of the target state as a tourist destination remains an important area of future research. In addition, it is also increasingly important to understand the role of sanctions in concert with other measures, such as consumer boycotts, with respect to change in the target. This is not only because the number of boycotts has grown markedly but also because boycotts appear to have a higher likelihood of success.

Do boycotts really work?

Boycotts as a vehicle for special-interest groups and ethical consumerism have grown in popularity, with a seemingly endless list of companies, movies, events, and more being shunned at any given time that are exposed to a wide range of concern of consumers (Watson, 2015). Clearly, boycotts are the preferred tool for consumers hoping to make their feelings known. Given the increasing awareness of consumers of their role as citizen in society, it is likely that more and more destinations, businesses, products, attractions, and individuals will be subjected to boycotts in the future in absolute if not relative terms. Tourism is no exception, and this can be observed in the wide range of boycotts employed by tourists, the majority of which are usually for non-tourism caused reasons (see Chapter 3).

The nature of our moral and ethical judgments and the extent to which we care about actions with respect to others depends in part on the distinctions we make between entities deemed worthy or unworthy of ethical and moral consideration – our moral boundaries (Crimston, Bain, Hornsey, & Bastian, 2016). Historically, human rights and politics were the main drivers for tourist boycotts, yet the range of rights concerns has expanded to include such concerns as LGBT rights in some countries, while environmental and animal welfare concerns have emerged as a mainstream phenomenon. The latter is often ignored despite the rise of massive societal concern across the world regarding animal treatment and is often specifically tourism focused at the attraction and destination level (Pacelle, 1993; Burghardt, 2009). The growth of boycotting can therefore, at least in part, be understood as an outcome of the spatial, i.e. beyond immediate community or country, and topical, i.e. as applied to a wider range of human and non-human subjects, expansion of ethical and moral concern, and empathy for others (Mills, 1994; Burghardt, 2009; Rollin, 2011; Bastian, Costello, Loughnan, & Hodson, 2012; Robison, 2014). As Rollin (2011, p. 103) observes:

> The last 50 years have witnessed a dazzling array of social ethical revolutions in Western society. Such moral movements as feminism, civil rights, environmentalism, affirmative action, consumer advocacy, pro- and anti-abortion activism, homosexual rights, children's rights, the student movement, antiwar activism, public rejection of biotechnology, have forever changed the way governments and public institutions comport themselves.

The expansion of ethical concern is closely connected to the growth in political consumerism as the markets of concerned consumption are based on the translation of moral values into tangible products and their purchase (buycotts) or rejection (boycott). The nature of the commercial market therefore changes through the expansion of moral concern (Brusdal & Frønes, 2013), with implications for the sender and the target of boycotts in both a tourism

---

Box 4.3 Transport for London bans advertisements from 11 countries over human rights

In May 2019 Transport for London (TfL) announced that it had suspended new advertisements from Saudi Arabia, Pakistan, and the United Arab Emirates while it carries out a review of countries with poor human rights records. TfL had run 26 advertising campaigns from countries with the death penalty for gay sex since October 2016 to May 2019. This included campaigns from Pakistan Tourism, Emirates airline, and Qatar Airways. Adverts promoting Brunei had already been removed from the TfL network after the country enacted laws punishing gay sex and adultery with death by stoning (see box 4.4). Eleven nations overall were suspended: Iran, Nigeria, Saudi Arabia, Somalia, Sudan, and Yemen have the death penalty for consensual sex between same-sex adults, while Pakistan, Qatar, the UAE, Mauritania, and Afghanistan have 'possible' death penalties according to the International Lesbian, Gay, Bisexual, Trans and Intersex Association (ILGA). A spokesman for Mayor Sadiq Khan said: 'Given the global role London plays championing LGBT+ rights, the Mayor has asked that TfL review how it treats advertising and sponsorship from countries with anti-LGBT+ laws' (quoted in Sleigh, 2019).

Source: Sleigh (2019)

---

and wider context (Box 4.3). Importantly, it can be argued that such change is not only concerned with the subject of boycotts but also the means by which ethical action is expressed.

Reflecting the shifting nature of boycotts as social and ethical concerns change, Shaheer et al. (2018) describe boycotts as social constructs and argue that the underlying reasons for boycotts are dynamic and are changing over time. This may pose some challenges for the target in the future as the dynamicity of boycotts affects the selection of coping and adaptation responses (Hall, Prayag, & Amore, 2017; Amore, Prayag, & Hall, 2018). Although, as noted in Chapter 3, transparency and openness appear to be key elements for a business in restricting the likelihood of being boycotted. Indeed, such a finding resonates well with the ethical justifications of boycotting. Beck (2019) in focusing on the role of consumer boycotts as instruments for structural change, concluded:

> well-designed consumer boycotts should be regarded as purposeful instruments for positive structural change, by which civil society agents can encourage corporations to live up to their responsibilities as moral agents, and communicate with a broad range of social agents who play different roles in bringing about the required transformation. . . . The leitmotiv for organised consumer boycotts should not be punishment and shaming of single business actors and their representatives. The focus should instead be ensuring long-term corporate compliance with justifiable normative principles, so that those frequently used concepts of 'corporate citizenship' and 'corporate social responsibility' will one day be a reality rather than empty words.
>
> (Beck, 2019, p. 557)

It is arguably much more difficult for tourism destinations to be able to respond to boycotts than businesses. This is because a destination is an amalgam of a wide range of different businesses, attractions, and attributes, each of which may give rise to a boycott event. As noted previously, it is usually not the destination per se that leads to a boycott but the association of the destination with things such as government actions and policies for which the destination becomes a target (Box 4.4), although destination management and marketing are not necessarily innocent from government actions. Nevertheless, tourism destinations need to develop an understanding not only of the triggering factors of boycotts but also suitable coping actions in an effort to minimize any future costs and repetitions. In seeking to identify responses to tourism crises and stereotypes, Avraham (2018) undertook a quantitative and qualitative content analysis of 70 advertisements produced in 47 countries, including print advertisements, television commercials, and YouTube videos. His analysis identified the use of three kinds of marketing strategies: source (personal testimony, blaming the media), message (expanding a narrow image, use of celebrities), and audience (emphasis on similar values, cultural symbols and geography, changing the target audience) (see also Avraham & Ketter, 2017; Tabak & Avraham, 2018).

Benoit's (1997, 2000, 2013, 2015a, 2015b) notion of image repair has been extremely influential with respect to how tourism destinations, attractions, and businesses can respond to boycotts. Image repair theory is based on two key assumptions. First, that communication is a goal-directed activity, i.e. it is conducted with a specific purpose and objective in mind. Second, that one of the central goals of communication is maintaining a positive image.

Box 4.4 Brunei says it will not enforce adultery and gay sex death penalty after boycott threats

In May 2019 Brunei's Sultan, Hassanal Bolkiah, announced the extension of a moratorium on the death penalty to incoming sharia penal code (SPCO) legislation on punishments for adultery and gay sex by stoning. This announcement followed a celebrity led call, including George Clooney, Elton John, and Ellen DeGeneres, for boycotting both Brunei and nine hotels in Europe and the USA owned by the sultan, including the Dorchester in London and the Beverley Hills hotel in Los Angeles (Guardian staff and agencies, 2019), as well as an advertising boycott on London public transport (Sleigh, 2019) (see Box 4.3). According to George Clooncy 'Let's be clear, every single time we stay at or take meetings at or dine at any of these nine hotels we are putting money directly into the pockets of men who choose to stone and whip to death their own citizens for being gay or accused of adultery' (The Guardian, 2019). In a speech before the start of the Islamic holy month of Ramadan the sultan said

> I am aware that there are many questions and misperceptions with regard to the implementation of the SPCO. However, we believe that once these have been cleared, the merit of the law will be evident. . . . As evident for more than two decades, we have practised a de facto moratorium on the execution of death penalty for cases under the common law. This will also be applied to cases under the SPCO, which provides a wider scope for remission.
>
> (quoted in Reuters, 2019)

Benoit (2015a) notes several strategies that are used to respond to crises (Table 4.1). Building on the work of Benoit, Avraham (2016, p. 42) suggests that destinations focus on three media strategy groups – source, audience, and message – with examples of their application in a number of different destination contexts (Avraham & Ketter, 2017; Tabak & Avraham, 2018):

- *source strategies* – focus on affecting or replacing the source believed by marketers to be responsible for the destination's negative image; e.g. by supplying stories and organizing familiarization tours for foreign journalists and media operating in key markets and/or by blocking media access;

Table 4.1 Corporate and destination image repair strategies

Strategy	Key characteristic	Examples
Denial		
Simple denial	Did not perform act; act occurred somewhere else	Business A, although sharing the same brand name as Business B, is 'innocent' because the targeted act of Business B occurred in another country
Shift the blame	Another performed act	Exxon in the wake of the Valdez oil spill on the Alaskan coastline (Dean, 2004); coral bleaching on the Great Barrier Reef is a result of global emissions not just Australia's
Evasion of responsibility		
Provocation/ scapegoating	Responded to act of another	Illegal immigration is a substantial problem which needs to be controlled (e.g. Gaynor, 2010b)
Defeasibility	Lack of information or ability	Brazilian government not to blame for Amazon deforestation
Accident	Mishap/mistake	Business claiming that the prevention of entry to someone from a visible minority was an accident
Good intentions	Meant well	Animal culls required for environmental management purposes
Reducing offensiveness of event		
Image bolstering	Stress good traits	In terms of BDS campaign Israel highlights that it is a democratic country in a region of non-democratic states (Cohen & Avraham, 2018)
Minimization	Act not serious	Brunei extension to moratorium on death penalty as punishments for gay sex (Box 4.4)
Differentiation	Act less offensive than similar acts	Indicating that this crisis is different from more offensive crises, i.e. animal welfare in destination A is better than in destination B
Transcendence	More important values	The cultural values of bullfighting or whaling are more important than animal welfare (Maria et al., 2017; Wearne, 2018)
Attack accuser	Reduce credibility of accuser	Israel accuses BDS campaign of being anti-semitic (Cohen & Avraham, 2018; Thrall, 2018)
Compensation	Reimburse victim	Making restitution to set things to where they were before the event. BP reimbursing tourism businesses affected by the Gulf oil spill (Greer & Best, 2016)
Corrective action	Plan to solve or prevent recurrence of event or problem	Improve corporate transparency
Mortification	Apologize/Admitting guilt and apologizing	Airbnb reversing its initial decision on delisting properties in illegal Israeli settlements (MEM, 2019)

Source: Strategies drawn from Benoit (2015a)

- *audience strategies* – deal with an audience's values, insights, and beliefs and are targeted by highlighting the commonalities between the values of the target destination or business and the foreign audience; and
- *message strategies* – aim to contradict negative perceptions about a destination or business, such as issues of risk and personal safety, or acceptance of minorities.

As noted in Chapter 3, such image repair strategies have been adopted by Israel in response to the BDS campaign at a global scale but particularly in Europe and the US because of their significance to Israel's strategic interests. Nevertheless, Israel has distinct advantages in terms of image repair as compared to a destination such as Myanmar as, unlike Israel, Myanmar has a lack of trained human resources, insufficient public services, and poor tourism infrastructure, which all complicate destination image beyond the long-term effects of a boycott (Hudson, 2016). Therefore, any consideration of destination image repair in a tourism context also needs to be connected with the potential for association between different influencing variables on destination image. In addition, such considerations also apply to private company responses to boycotts (Dean, 2004; Greer & Best, 2016).

Social media, boycotts, and communication

Technological innovations with respect to social media and the widespread use and accessibility of the Internet have spurred the growth of boycotts as they provide not only a wide variety of technical tools for self-expression or mass communication originated by individuals but also enable public discussion and citizen participation (McDonnell & King, 2013; De Zúñiga, Copeland, & Bimber, 2014). This can be seen in the growing role of social media which provide convenient platforms for spreading the call for a boycott at the lowest cost. Becker and Copeland (2016) found that LGBT users of social media for connective activities (e.g. meet new friends, discuss issues) are significantly more likely to engage in boycotts or buycotts to promote equality and conclude that 'connective social media use mobilizes people with low levels of political interest to participate and reinforces the likelihood that people with high levels of political interest participate' (Becker & Copeland, 2016, p. 22). They also note that their results suggest that LGBT individuals who engage in political consumerism are not all that different from US political consumers in general. Hitchcock (2016) is more cautious in her study of social media and boycott behavior and suggests that social media discourse does not necessarily generate the same level of emotional connection or interactivity with audiences as other media or personal connectivity. Furthermore, from a German study Kelm and Dohle (2018) suggest that online communication mediates the influence of online information on boycotts and buycotts but that boycotts are more influenced by communication activities than buycotts.

Ruijgrok (2017) argues that the growth of the Internet and its growing accessibility has facilitated the occurrence of protests in authoritarian regimes, because the use of the Internet has increased access to information in such regimes despite attempts to control cyberspace. This is what has been called 'online activism' and was witnessed in protests and people mobilizations such as Arab Spring and the Occupy movement. This mainstream phenomenon is believed to alter the landscape of the practice of protest and consumer boycott regimes (AlSayyad & Guvenc, 2015). Nevertheless, the utility and effectiveness of social media is subjected to debate. Wolfsfeld, Segev, and Sheafer (2013, p. 117) explain that:

> The cyber-enthusiasts express optimism about the ability of the new media to empower people living in nondemocratic societies and to allow insurgents to adopt new strategies . . . .The cyber-skeptics downplay the significance of the new technology, arguing that using the Internet gives people a false sense of participation and keeps them from actual physical protesting. Some cyber-skeptics have even argued that the new media are tools of repression.

Miller (2017), for example, challenges the claims of digital-and cyber-enthusiasts with respect to the role of social media in expanding political consumerism. Instead, he suggests that digital politics demonstrates a rise of 'phatic communion' – promote social harmony through the maintenance of relationships – in social media, which has atrophied the potential for digital communications technologies to foster social change. Indeed, Endres and Panagopoulos (2017), using two nationally-representative surveys and a survey of registered voters, found Americans' engagement in boycotts and buycotts for political or social reasons to be widespread. However while social media was important, other factors such as political knowledge, ideological intensity, and an interest in politics were also significantly associated with political behavior. This interest in the influence of social media on boycott behavior shares some strong linkages with research on the use of upstream social marketing in tourism and related areas, such as conservation, to encourage structural change (Hall, 2016; Mehmet & Simmons, 2019). Nevertheless, given the clear overlap between boycotts and buycotts and the use of social media in tourism, it is clear that the role of digital technologies in contributing to consumer activism in a tourism context should be a significant area of future research.

Conclusion: sanctions and boycotts in an interconnected world

As this book has demonstrated, the number of sanctions and boycotts has increased substantially since the 1980s. Such change is closely related to various aspects of globalization including changes in the international political order, the development of new communications technology, the expansion of international trade and finance, and the growth of international environmental, consumer, and human rights movements. Greater interconnectivity has meant that sanctions and boycotts are often regarded as ready-made tools to influence the actions and behaviors of countries, destinations, and businesses, although, as this book has demonstrated, boycotts appear to be more successful in achieving change than sanctions. Nevertheless, it is often the perception of appropriateness and effectiveness that is important in the selection of sanctions, rather than the reality.

Greater connectivity together with the expansion of areas that have become relevant for economic statecraft and political consumerism means that the range of topics that become significant for boycotts has grown substantially. While the 1970s saw calls for tourism boycotts on the basis of race and political oppression, these concerns, while still very relevant, have been added to with concern for minority rights growing to include the LGBT community and various cultural and ethnic groups, including First Peoples. Although more limited to domestic contexts, there is also greater concern for labor conditions and the need for a living wage in the tourism and hospitality sector (McDonnell, 2010). In addition, the environment has continued to expand as an area of political consumerism and has also extended to tourist concern over animal rights.

The growing challenge of climate change as a significant global concern, has paved the ground for the potential for boycotts and some even called for 'an Apartheid-style boycott' on inefficient products to help save the planet (Tutu, 2014). The rationale behind this is to encourage those countries and companies primarily responsible for emitting carbon and accelerating climate change to transition to a low-carbon economy. Tourism is increasingly becoming a focus of climate change campaigns, especially because of the emissions from aviation and cruise ships. Climate change NGOs have already been influential with carbon divestment campaigns as well as energy companies, banks, and insurers (Roser-Renouf, Atkinson, Maibach, & Leiserowitz, 2016; Ballew, Goldberg, Rosenthal, Cutler, & Leiserowitz, 2019). Activists such as Greta Thunberg have led to the growth of 'flygskam/flying shame', leading to a growth in train travel and a decline in air travel in Sweden and having a wider influence in encouraging consumers to think about their journeys (Hoikkala &

Magnusson, 2019). Such actions are also increasingly complimented by opposition to airport runway development and other travel infrastructure. Indeed, Extinction Rebellion, a significant element of the global climate change protest movement, which as of August 2019 had over 100,000 members on its database and operates in 59 countries, stemmed from a failed protest over bus lane development on a treed allotment in Bristol, UK (BBC News, 2019b).

While consumer activism is important with respect to the environment, growing concern over global heating means that global environmental change and biodiversity conservation are gradually becoming part of foreign policy concerns and economic diplomacy. For example, Brazil and its far-right president, Jair Bolsonaro's belligerent response to international concerns over fires in the Amazon in 2019 led to asset managers, pension funds, and companies halting deals and stopping buying bonds, calls for boycotts, and a potential delay in the ratification of a trade deal between the South American trade block Mercosur and the EU (Phillips, 2019). According to Fabio Silveira, a director and partner at Macrosector, a São Paulo financial consulting firm, 'The disaster has already been done to the environmental image. . . . That means that the cost lenders put on Brazil's environmental risk, previously regarded as close to zero, just went up. . . . Brazilian companies and the Brazilian government lose. Nobody can deny international banks put a cost on environmental risk' (quoted in Phillips, 2019).

Boycotts and sanctions as the new ethical tourism?

Ethics now occupies an important place in the choice of destination and tourism product, and it can also be reflected in how tourists practice political and ethical consumerism in their travel. Boycotting, not boycotting or even buycotting attractions, brands, and destinations has become an increasingly common debate among tourists. While there is one view that we should avoid at all costs to go to a country where human or animal rights are violated in order not to condone the abuses, the opponents of such a view believe that going to such destinations might help to get the population out of their isolation. There are no easy answers. Nevertheless, it is clear that boycotts and sanctions are increasingly a part of the ethics of tourism, whether in terms of their effects or their capacity to generate positive change.

The ethics of tourism has long been concerned with what tourists purchase and the effect of tourism on communities and the environment. Indeed, the growth of concern over the expansion of tourism in many destinations and the displacement of permanent residents is itself creating the potential for boycotts of tourism. However, ethical considerations have now been extended to a range of areas that affect tourism and hospitality and which consumers, interest groups, industry, and policy makers are now engaging with, even if in some cases the conduct of boycotts and sanctions means that they have no choice. Perhaps most importantly of all, ethical boycotts and sanctions are grounded in broader considerations of community and commonwealth and arise from obligations to stand in solidarity with those who are affected by bad actors and give direction to injustice (Fischer, 2019). Although we fully acknowledge that some sanctions in particular only serve a narrow self-interest and do not meet normative ethical principles, we would suggest that actions grounded in community membership, relationships, and identifying with others – our common humanity and planet – provide a sound basis to frame the ethicality of sanctions, boycotts, and, of course, tourism.

References

Abosag, I., & Farah, M. (2014). The influence of religiously motivated consumer boycotts on brand image, loyalty and product judgment. *European Journal of Marketing, 48*(11/12), 2262–2283.

AFP. (2019). US to deny visas for ICC members investigating alleged war crimes. *The Guardian*, 15 March. Retrieved from www.theguardian.com/us-news/2019/mar/15/mike-pompeo-us-war-crimes-investigation-international-criminal-court

AFP in Geneva. (2019). UN rights chief decries latest US sanctions targeting Venezuela. *The Guardian*, 9 August. Retrieved from www.theguardian.com/world/2019/aug/09/un-rights-chief-decries-latest-us-sanctions-venezuela-michelle-bachelet

Alexander, K. (2009). *Economic sanctions: Law and public policy.* London: Palgrave Macmillan.

Al-Hyari, K., Alnsour, M., Al-Weshah, G., & Haffar, M. (2012). Religious beliefs and consumer behaviour: From loyalty to boycotts. *Journal of Islamic Marketing, 3*(2), 155–174.

Alipour, H., & Kilic, H. (2005). An institutional appraisal of tourism development and planning: The case of the Turkish Republic of North Cyprus (TRNC). *Tourism Management, 26*(1), 79–94.

Allagui, S. (2006). Danish business feels the pain of cartoon boycotts. Retrieved from https://web.archive.org/web/20060717193324/www.middle-east-online.com/english/business/?id=15795

Allen, S. H. (2008a). Political institutions and constrained response to economic sanctions. *Foreign Policy Analysis, 4*(3), 255–274.

Allen, S. H. (2008b). The domestic political costs of economic sanctions. *Journal of Conflict Resolution, 52*(6), 916–944.

Alper, D. K. (1997). Transboundary environmental relations in British Columbia and the Pacific Northwest. *American Review of Canadian Studies, 27*(3), 359–383.

AlSayyad, N., & Guvenc, M. (2015). Virtual uprisings: On the interaction of new social media, traditional media coverage and urban space during the "Arab Spring". *Urban Studies, 52*(11), 2018–2034.

Amnesty International. (2019). Destination: Occupation. Retrieved from www.amnesty.org/en/latest/campaigns/2019/01/destination-occupation-digital-tourism-israel-illegal-settlements/

Amore, A., Prayag, G., & Hall, C. M. (2018). Conceptualizing destination resilience from a multilevel perspective. *Tourism Review International*, *22*(3–4), 235–250.

Aratani, L. (2019). Equinox and SoulCycle face boycott over investor's Trump fundraiser. *The Guardian*, 8 August. Retrieved from www.theguardian.com/us-news/2019/aug/07/equinox-soulcycle-trump-fundraiser-stephen-ross

Aridan, N. (2017). *Advocating for Israel: Diplomats and lobbyists from Truman to Nixon*. Lanham, MA: Lexington Books.

Arnold, J. E. (1995). Social inequality, marginalization, and economic process. In T. D. Price & G. M. Feinman (Eds.), *Foundations of social inequality* (pp. 87–103). New York, NY: Plenum.

Attanapola, C. T., & Lund, R. (2013). Contested identities of indigenous people: Indigenization or integration of the Veddas in Sri Lanka. *Singapore Journal of Tropical Geography*, *34*(2), 172–187.

Avraham, E. (2016). Destination marketing and image repair during tourism crises: The case of Egypt. *Journal of Hospitality and Tourism Management*, *28*, 41–48.

Avraham, E. (2018). Nation branding and marketing strategies for combatting tourism crises and stereotypes toward destinations. *Journal of Business Research*. doi:10.1016/j.jbusres.2018.02.036

Avraham, E., & Ketter, E. (2017). Destination marketing during and following crises: Combating negative images in Asia. *Journal of Travel & Tourism Marketing*, *34*(6), 709–718.

Axelrod, T. (2018). Iran: US sanctions are "economic terrorism". *The Hill*. Retrieved from https://thehill.com/policy/international/middle-east-north-africa/408356-iran-us-sanctions-are-economic-terrorism

Bærenholdt, J. O. (2013). Governmobility: The powers of mobility. *Mobilities*, *8*(1), 20–34.

Ballew, M. T., Goldberg, M. H., Rosenthal, S. A., Cutler, M. J., & Leiserowitz, A. (2019). Climate change activism among Latino and white Americans. *Frontiers in Communication*, *3*, 58.

Baptista, J. A. (2012). The virtuous tourist: Consumption, development, and non-governmental governance in a Mozambican village. *American Anthropologist*, *114*(4), 639–651.

Barbieri, K., Keshk, O. M. G., & Pollins, B. (2009). Trading data: Evaluating our assumptions and coding rules. *Conflict Management and Peace Science*, *26*(5), 471–491.

Barghouti, O. (2019). I co-founded the BDS movement: Why was I denied entry to the US? With this denial of entry, Israel appears to have once again enlisted the Trump administration to do its bidding. *The Guardian*, 16 April. Retrieved from www.theguardian.com/commentisfree/2019/apr/16/bds-movement-omar-barghouti-denied-entry

Barinaga, M. (1991). Abortion stirs the neuroscience gumbo: A flap is developing over whether neuroscientists should boycott Louisiana because of the state's strict abortion law. *Science*, *254*(5031), 514.

Bassett, K., & Hoare, T. (1987). Sanctions against South Africa: Some regional and local dimensions of the national debate. *Area*, 303–312.

Bastian, B., Costello, K., Loughnan, S., & Hodson, G. (2012). When closing the human-animal divide expands moral concern: The importance of framing. *Social Psychological and Personality Science*, *3*(4), 421–429.

Bayer, L. (2016). The geopolitics of sanctions. *Geopolitical Futures*. Abingdon: Routledge. Retrieved from https://geopoliticalfutures.com/the-geopolitics-of-sanctions/

BBC News. (2006). *Cartoons row hits Danish exports*. BBC News, 9 September. Retrieved from http://news.bbc.co.uk/2/hi/europe/5329642.stm

BBC News. (2019a). Chinese films banned from joining Taiwan's Golden Horse Awards. *BBC News*, 7 August. Retrieved from www.bbc.com/news/world-asia-49260342

BBC News. (2019b). Extinction Rebellion "stemmed from failed bus lane protest". *BBC News*, 1 September. Retrieved from www.bbc.com/news/uk-england-49513802

BDS. (2019). *What is BDS?* Retrieved from https://bdsmovement.net/what-is-bds

Beck, V. (2019). Consumer boycotts as instruments for structural change. *Journal of Applied Philosophy*, *36*(4), 543–559.

Becker, A. B., & Copeland, L. (2016). Networked publics: How connective social media use facilitates political consumerism among LGBT Americans. *Journal of Information Technology & Politics*, *13*(1), 22–36.

Benoit, W. L. (1997). Image repair discourse and crisis communication. *Public Relations Review*, *23*(2), 177–186.

Benoit, W. L. (2000). Another visit to the theory of image restoration strategies. *Communication Quarterly*, *48*(1), 40–43.

Benoit, W. L. (2013). Image repair theory and corporate reputation. In C. E. Carroll (Ed.), *The handbook of communication and corporate reputation* (pp. 213–221). Malden, MA: Wiley Blackwell.

Benoit, W. L. (2015a). Image repair theory in the context of strategic communication. In D. Holtzhausen & A. Zerfass (Eds.), *The Routledge handbook of strategic communication* (pp. 303–311). Abingdon: Routledge.

Benoit, W. L. (2015b). *Accounts, excuses, apologies: Image repair theory and research* (2nd edn.). Albany: State University of New York Press.

Bertulli, C. G., Leeney, R. H., Barreau, T., & Matassa, D. S. (2016). Can whale-watching and whaling co-exist? Tourist perceptions in Iceland. *Journal of the Marine Biological Association of the United Kingdom*, *96*(4), 969–977.

Bey, M. (2018). The U.S. supersizes its sanctions. *Stratfor*. Retrieved from https://worldview.stratfor.com/article/us-supersizes-its-sanctions

Bezhan, F. (2017). Flight fight: Proposed tripling of "departure tax" roils Iranians. Retrieved from www.rferl.org/a/iran-skyrocketing-departure-tax-proposal-anger-tourism/28914103.html

Bhungalia, L. (2010). A liminal territory: Gaza, executive discretion, and sanctions turned humanitarian. *GeoJournal*, *75*(4), 347–357.

Bidwell, D. (2009). Bison, boundaries, and brucellosis: Risk perception and political ecology at Yellowstone. *Society & Natural Resources*, *23*(1), 14–30.

Biersteker, T. J., Eckert, S., Tourinho, M., & Hudáková, Z. (2013). *The effectiveness of United Nations targeted sanctions: Findings from the targeted sanctions consortium*. Geneva: Graduate Institute for International Studies.

Biersteker, T. J., Tourinho, M., & Eckert, S. E. (2016). Thinking about United Nations targeted sanctions. In T. J. Biersteker, S. E. Eckert, & M. Tourinho (Eds.), *Targeted sanctions: The impacts and effectiveness of United Nations action* (pp. 11–37). Cambridge: Cambridge University Press.

Bisharat, G. (2001). Sanctions as genocide. *Transnational Law and Contemporary Problems, 11,* 379.

Blair, G. (2019). South Korean petrol stations refuse to fill up Japanese cars amid growing boycott. *The Guardian,* 24 July. Retrieved from www.theguardian.com/world/2019/jul/24/south-korean-petrol-stations-refuse-to-fill-up-japanese-cars-amid-growing-boycott

Boffey, D. (2019). UN court judge quits The Hague citing political interference. *The Guardian,* 28 January. Retrieved from www.theguardian.com/law/2019/jan/28/international-criminal-court-icc-judge-christoph-flugge-quits-citing-political-interference-trump-administration-turkey

Boogaerts, A. (2018). An effective sanctioning actor? Merging effectiveness and EU actorness criteria to explain evolutions in (in) effective coercion towards Iran. *European Security, 27*(2), 138–157.

Bowcott, O. (2019). ICC rejects request to investigate war crimes in Afghanistan. *The Guardian,* 12 April. Retrieved from www.theguardian.com/law/2019/apr/12/icc-rejects-request-to-investigate-war-crimes-in-afghanistan

Branigan, T., & Hale, E. (2019). Cathay denounced for firing Hong Kong staff after pressure from China. *The Guardian,* 28 August. Retrieved from www.theguardian.com/world/2019/aug/28/cathay-pacific-denounced-for-firing-hong-kong-staff-on-china-orders

Braunsberger, K., & Buckler, B. (2011). What motivates consumers to participate in boycotts: Lessons from the ongoing Canadian seafood boycott. *Journal of Business Research, 64*(1), 96–102.

Bray, J. (2002). Burma: The dilemmas of commercial and humanitarian engagement. *Corporate Environmental Strategy, 9*(2), 155–162.

Brewer, M. B., & Brown, R. J. (1998). Intergroup relations. In D. T. Gilbert, S. T. Fiske, & G. Lindzey (Eds.), *The handbook of social psychology* (pp. 554–594). Boston: McGraw-Hill.

Brusdal, R., & Frønes, I. (2013). The purchase of moral positions: An essay on the markets of concerned parenting. *International Journal of Consumer Studies, 37*(2), 159–164.

Brzoska, M. (2003). From dumb to smart-recent reforms of UN sanctions. *Global Governance, 9,* 519–535.

Brzoska, M. (2015). International sanctions before and beyond UN sanctions. *International Affairs, 91*(6), 1339–1349.

Burghardt, G. M. (2009). Ethics and animal consciousness: How rubber the ethical ruler? *Journal of Social Issues, 65*(3), 499–521.

Cameron, I. (2003). UN targeted sanctions, legal safeguards and the European Convention on Human Rights. *Nordic Journal of International Law, 72*(2), 159–214.

Canavan, B. (2018). Your choice of holiday destination is a political act. *The Independent,* 6 August. Retrieved from www.independent.co.uk/voices/holiday-choice-politics-where-go-ethics-israel-cuba-china-taiwan-dubai-a8479231.html

Care 2. (2019). Boycott Kerala tourism to save animal slaughter. Retrieved from www.thepetitionsite.com/fr-fr/1/boycott-kerala-tourism-to-save-animal-slaughter/

Carneiro, C., & Apolinário, L., Jr. (2016). Targeted versus conventional economic sanctions: What is at stake for human rights? *International Interactions, 42*(4), 565–589.

Carter, N. (2018). *The politics of the environment: Ideas, activism, policy.* Cambridge: Cambridge University Press.

Caruana, R. (2007). A sociological perspective of consumption morality. *Journal of Consumer Behaviour, 6*(5), 287–304.

Caruana, R., & Crane, A. (2011). Getting away from it all: Exploring freedom in tourism. *Annals of Tourism Research, 38*(4), 1495–1515.

Castaneda, Q., & Burtner, J. (2010). Tourism as "a Force for World Peace": The politics of tourism, tourism as governmentality and the tourism boycott of Guatemala. *The Journal of Tourism and Peace Research, 1*(2), 1–21.

Castelló, E., & Mihelj, S. (2018). Selling and consuming the nation: Understanding consumer nationalism. *Journal of Consumer Culture, 18*(4), 558–576.

Cetin, H., Akmese, H., Aras, S., & Aytekin, V. (2016). The effects of the Russian crisis on Turkish tourism sector: A case of Antalya Province, Turkey. *International Journal of Social, Behavioral, Educational, Economic, Business and Industrial Engineering, 10*(7), 2566–2570.

Chatzidakis, A., & Lee, M. S. (2013). Anti-consumption as the study of reasons against. *Journal of Macromarketing, 33*(3), 190–203.

Cho, S., & Krasser, A. H. (2011). What makes us care? The impact of cultural values, individual factors, and attention to media content on motivation for ethical consumerism. *International Social Science Review, 86*(1/2), 3–23.

Christopher, A. J. (1994). The pattern of diplomatic sanctions against South Africa 1948–1994. *GeoJournal, 34*(4), 439–446.

Chung-Min, T. (2019). Taiwan in 2018: A bitter campaign and an uncertain future. *Asian Survey, 59*(1), 77–84.

Cohen, R., & Avraham, E. (2018). North American Jewish NGOs and strategies used in fighting BDS and the boycott of Israeli academia. *Israel Studies, 23*(2), 194–216.

Coles, T. E. (2008). Citizenship and the state: Hidden features in the internationalization of tourism. In T. E. Coles & C. M. Hall (Eds.), *International business and tourism: Global issues, contemporary interactions* (pp. 55–69). Abingdon: Routledge.

Coles, T. E., & Hall, C. M. (Eds.). (2008). *International business and tourism: Global issues, contemporary interactions.* Abingdon: Routledge.

Connell, J. (2017). Shining light on the darkness: Placing tourists within North Korean tourism: Comment on: Desiring the dark: "A taste for the unusual" in North Korean tourism? *Current Issues in Tourism, 20*(4), 356–362.

Connolly, R. (2018). *Russia's response to sanctions: How Western economic statecraft is reshaping political economy in Russia.* Cambridge: Cambridge University Press.

Corporate Critic: Ethical Consumer Research Association. (2018). What is corporate critic. Retrieved from www.corporatecritic.org/home.aspx

Cortright, D., & Lopez, G. A. (2000). *The sanctions decade: Assessing UN strategies in the 1990s*. Boulder: Lynne Rienner.

Cortright, D., & Lopez, G. A. (2002). *Smart sanctions: Targeting economic statecraft and international relations*. New York: Rowman & Littlefield.

Cortright, D., & Lopez, G. A. (2018a). *Economic sanctions: Panacea or peacebuilding in a post-cold war world?* Abingdon: Routledge.

Cortright, D., & Lopez, G. A. (2018b). Research concerns and policy needs in an era of sanctions. In D. Cortright & G. A. Lopez (Eds.), *Economic sanctions: Panacea or peacebuilding in a post-cold war world?* (pp. 201–208). Abingdon: Routledge.

Council of the European Union. (2019). EU sanctions map. Retrieved from www.sanctionsmap.eu/#/main

Coville, T. (2018). Quel sens donner à l'économie de la résistance ? [What is the meaning of the economy of resistance?]. *La Revue de Téhéran*. Retrieved from www.teheran.ir/spip.php?article2494#gsc.tab=0

Crawford, N. C. (1999). Trump card or theater? An introduction to two sanctions debates. In N. C. Crawford & A. Klotz (Eds.), *How sanctions work: Lessons from South Africa* (pp. 3–24). Basingstoke: MacMillan.

Crimston, D., Bain, P. G., Hornsey, M. J., & Bastian, B. (2016). Moral expansiveness: Examining variability in the extension of the moral world. *Journal of Personality and Social Psychology, 111*(4), 636–653.

Crossley, J. G. (2011). Life of Brian or life of Jesus? Uses of critical biblical scholarship and non-orthodox views of Jesus in Monty Python's *Life of Brian. Relegere: Studies in Religion and Reception, 1*(1), 93–114.

Crouzet, F. (1964). Wars, blockade, and economic change in Europe, 1792–1815. *The Journal of Economic History, 24*(4), 567–588.

Crumley, B. (2004). After the head-scarf ban. *Time International (South Pacific Edition), 7*, 40.

Cruz, B. D. P. A. (2017). Social boycott. *Revista Brasileira de Gestão de Negócios, 19*(63), 5–29.

Dajani, M. S., & Daoudi, M. (1983). *Economic sanctions, ideals and experience*. London: Routledge and Kegan Paul.

Dalby, S. (2013). The geopolitics of climate change. *Political Geography, 37*, 38–47.

Dalton, H. (2019). *Towards the peace of nations: A study in international politics*. London: Routledge.

Dalton, R. J. (2008). Citizenship norms and the expansion of political participation. *Political Studies, 56*(1), 76–98.

Davidson, D. K. (1995). Ten tips for boycott targets. *Business Horizons, 38*(2), 77–80.

Davies, P. R. (2004). *Whose bible is it anyway?* (2nd edn.). London: T&T Clark International.

Dean, D. H. (2004). Consumer reaction to negative publicity: Effects of corporate reputation, response, and responsibility for a crisis event. *The Journal of Business Communication, 41*(2), 192–211.

De Crespigny, A. R. C., & McKinnel, R. T. (1960). The nature and significance of economic boycott. *South African Journal of Economics, 28*(4), 319–336.

De Goede, M. (2011). Blacklisting and the ban: Contesting targeted sanctions in Europe. *Security Dialogue, 42*(6), 499–515.

Dehghan, S. K. (2015). Iran threatens Frankfurt book fair boycott over Rushdie speech. *The Guardian,* 6 October. Retrieved from www.theguardian.com/books/2015/oct/06/iran-threatens-frankfurt-book-fair-boycott-over-rushdie-speech

Delacote, P. (2009). On the sources of consumer boycotts ineffectiveness. *The Journal of Environment & Development, 18*(3), 306–322.

De Zúñiga, H. G., Copeland, L., & Bimber, B. (2014). Political consumerism: Civic engagement and the social media connection. *New Media & Society, 16*(3), 488–506.

Doxey, M. (1990). International sanctions. In D. Gahlunds & M. Hawes (Eds.), *World politics, power interdependence and dependence.* Toronto: Harcourt Brace Jovanovich, Toronto.

Dreyer, I., & Popescu, N. (2014). *Do sanctions against Russia work?* European Union Institute for Security Studies 35. Paris: European Union Institute for Security Studies.

Drezner, D. W. (2015). Targeted sanctions in a world of global finance. *International Interactions, 41*(4), 755–764.

Drezner, D. W., & Drezner, D. W. (1999). *The sanctions paradox: Economic statecraft and international relations.* Cambridge: Cambridge University Press.

Early, B. R. (2015). *Busted sanctions: Explaining why economic sanctions fail.* Stanford, CA: Stanford University Press.

Encyclopedia Britannica. (2019). Boycott. Retrieved from www.britannica.com/topic/boycott

Endres, K., & Panagopoulos, C. (2017). Boycotts, buycotts, and political consumerism in America. *Research & Politics, 4*(4). doi:10.1177/2053168017738632

Esfandiari, G. (2012). Iran looks to "resistive economy" to fight sanctions. *Radio Free Europe,* 12 August. Retrieved from www.rferl.org/a/iran-looks-to-resistive-economy-to-fight-sanctions/24674314.html

Essoo, N., & Dibb, S. (2004). Religious influences on shopping behaviour: An exploratory study. *Journal of Marketing Management, 20*(7–8), 683–712.

Ettenson, R., & Klein, J. G. (2005). The fallout from French nuclear testing in the South Pacific: A longitudinal study of consumer boycotts. *International Marketing Review, 22*(2), 199–224.

European Commission. (2019). Sanctions. Retrieved from https://ec.europa.eu/fpi/what-we-do/sanctions_en

European Council. (2019). Sanctions: How and when the EU adopts restrictive measures. Retrieved from www.consilium.europa.eu/en/policies/sanctions/

Eyler, R. (2007). *Economic sanctions: International policy and political economy at work.* London: Palgrave Macmillan.

Fanusie, Y. (2018). Blockchain authoritarianism: The regime in iran goes crypto. *The Forbes.* Retrieved from www.forbes.com/sites/yayafanusie/2018/08/15/blockchain-authoritarianism-the-regime-in-iran-goes-crypto/#7733591d3dc6

Farah, M. F., & Newman, A. J. (2010). Exploring consumer boycott intelligence using a socio-cognitive approach. *Journal of Business Research, 63*(4), 347–355.

Farahani, B. M. & Shabani, M. (2013). The impact of sanctions on Iran's tourism. *The Open Access Journal of Resistive Economics* (OAJRE), 33, 1–13.

Farrall, J. M. (2007). *United Nations sanctions and the rule of law*. Cambridge: Cambridge University Press.

Fennell, D. A. (2012). Tourism and animal rights. *Tourism Recreation Research*, *37*(2), 157–166.

Financial Tribune. (2018a). Iran government's departure tax revenues rise 178%. Retrieved from https://financialtribune.com/articles/travel/94722/iran-governments-departure-tax-revenues-rise-178

Financial Tribune. (2018b). Iran boosts marine tourism to attract more foreign travelers. Retrieved from https://financialtribune.com/articles/economy-travel/94138/iran-boosts-marine-tourism-to-attract-more-foreign-travelers

Fischer, B. (2019). *Boycotting and public mourning*, Res Publica, https://doi.org/10.1007/s11158-019-09419-2

Fischhendler, I., Herman, L., & Maoz, N. (2017). The political economy of energy sanctions: Insights from a global outlook 1938–2017. *Energy Research & Social Science, 34*, 62–71.

Fisk, D. W. (2000). Economic sanctions: The Cuba embargo revisited. In S. Chan & A. Cooper Drury (Eds.), *Sanctions as economic statecraft: Theory and practice* (pp. 65–85). London: Palgrave Macmillan.

Forbes. (2018). The $1 trillion marketing executives are ignoring. Retrieved from www.forbes.com/sites/debtfreeguys/2018/08/14/the-1-trillion-marketing-executives-are-ignoring/#a405c65a97f2

Frank, R. (2006). The political economy of sanctions against North Korea. *Asian Perspective, 20*(3), 5–36.

Freeman, C. P., Bekoff, M., & Bexell, S. M. (2011). Giving voice to the "voiceless" incorporating nonhuman animal perspectives as journalistic sources. *Journalism Studies, 12*(5), 590–607.

Freeman, J. R. (2018). *Artists and activism: Black voices of resistance and the cultural boycott of South Africa*. PhD. Purdue University.

Friedman, M. (1991). Consumer boycotts: A conceptual framework and research agenda. *Journal of Social Issues, 47*(1), 149–168.

Friedman, M. (1995). American consumer boycotts in response to rising food prices: Housewives' protests at the grassroots level. *Journal of Consumer Policy, 18*(1), 55–72.

Friedman, M. (1999). *Consumer boycotts: Effecting change through the marketplace and media*. New York: Routledge.

Friedman, M. (2004). Using consumer boycotts to stimulate corporate policy changes: Marketplace, media, and moral considerations. In M. Micheletti, A. Follesdal, & D. Stolle (Eds.), *Politics, products and markets: Exploring political consumerism past and present* (pp. 45–62). New Brunswick, NJ: Transaction Publishers.

Gaffney, C. (2013). Between discourse and reality: The un-sustainability of mega-event planning. *Sustainability, 5*(9), 3926–3940.

Gallego, A. (2007). *Inequality in political participation: Contemporary patterns in European countries*. CSD Working Papers. Irvine, CA: UC Irvine, Center for the Study of Democracy.

Galtung, J. (1967). On the effects of international economic sanctions, with examples from the case of Rhodesia. *World Politics*, *19*(3), 378–416.

García-de-Frutos, N., Ortega-Egea, J. M., & Martínez-del-Río, J. (2018). Anti-consumption for environmental sustainability: Conceptualization, review, and multilevel research directions. *Journal of Business Ethics*, *148*(2), 411–435.

Gardberg, N., & Newburry, W. (2009). Who boycotts whom? Marginalization, company knowledge, and strategic issues. *Business & Society*, *52*(2), 318–357.

Garrett, D. E. (1987). The effectiveness of marketing policy boycotts: Environmental opposition to marketing. *Journal of Marketing*, *51*(2), 46–57.

Gartner, W. C., & Shen, J. (1992). The impact of Tiananmen Square on China's tourism image. *Journal of Travel Research*, *30*(4), 47–52.

Gaynor, T. (2010a). Immigration law boycott cost Ariz. $140 mln: Study. *Reuters*, 19 November. Retrieved from www.reuters.com/article/us-arizona-boycott-idUSTRE6AH55W20101118

Gaynor, T. (2010b). Republicans target birthright citizenship for illegal immigrants' children. *Reuters*, 4 August. Retrieved from http://blogs.reuters.com/talesfromthetrail/2010/08/04/2010/08/04/republicans-target-birthright-citizenship-for-illegal-immigrants-children/

Gilbert, J. (2014). *Nomadic peoples and human rights*. London: Routledge.

Gille, Z. (2011). The Hungarian foie gras boycott: Struggles for moral sovereignty in postsocialist Europe. *East European Politics and Societies*, *25*(1), 114–128.

Gilsinan, K. (2019). A boom time for U.S. sanctions. Retrieved from www.theatlantic.com/politics/archive/2019/05/why-united-states-uses-sanctions-so-much/588625/

Girit, S. (2016). Turkey faces big losses as Russia sanctions bite. *BBC News, Istanbul*, 2 January. Retrieved from www.bbc.com/news/world-europe-35209987

Glaesser, D. (2006). *Crisis management in the tourism industry*. London: Routledge.

Goldberg, E. (2019). Trump and Netanyahu are playing a bigoted game of chicken. *The Guardian*, 17 August. Retrieved from www.theguardian.com/commentisfree/2019/aug/17/trump-netanyahu-ilhan-omar-rashida-tlaib

Gordon, J. (1999). Sanctions as siege warfare. *Nation*, *268*(11), 18–21.

Gordon, J. (2016). Economic sanctions as "negative development": The case of Cuba. *Journal of International Development*, *28*(4), 473–484.

Grauvogel, J., & von Soest, C. (2013). *Claims to legitimacy matter: Why sanctions fail to instigate democratization in authoritarian regimes*. GIGA Working Papers No. 235. Hamburg: German Institute of Global and Area Studies (GIGA).

Greer, A., & Best, E. (2016). Size doesn't matter: The complicated relationship between national offshore oil spill events, framing, and policy. *International Journal of Mass Emergencies & Disasters*, *34*(1), 25–46.

The Guardian. (2017). Editorial: The Guardian view on sanctions: An essential tool. *The Guardian*, 6 August. Retrieved from www.theguardian.com/commentisfree/2017/aug/06/the-guardian-view-on-sanctions-an-essential-tool

The Guardian. (2019). Judo star left fearing for safety after defying orders from Iran. *The Guardian*, 2 September. Retrieved from www.theguardian.com/world/2019/sep/02/judo-star-left-fearing-for-life-after-defying-orders-from-iran

Guardian sport and agencies. (2019). US Olympic medalist faces discipline for taking knee after winning Pan-Am gold. *The Guardian*, 11 August. Retrieved from www.theguardian.com/sport/2019/aug/10/race-imboden-kneels-national-anthem-pan-am-games

Guardian staff and agencies. (2019). Celebrities boycott Brunei-owned hotels over country's new anti-LGBT laws. *The Guardian*, 4 April. Retrieved from www.theguardian.com/world/2019/apr/03/brunei-lgbt-stoning-boycotts

Gurvich, E., & Prilepskiy, I. (2016). The impact of financial sanctions on the Russian economy. *Voprosy economiki, 1*.

Hahn, T. (2018). Why consumers boycott even if prospects look bleak. *Forbes*, 16 October. Retrieved from www.forbes.com/sites/esade/2018/10/16/why-consumers-boycott-even-if-prospects-look-bleak/#435cee014910

Hahn, T., & Albert, N. (2017). Strong reciprocity in consumer boycotts. *Journal of Business Ethics, 145*(3), 509–524.

Haidar, J. I. (2017). Sanctions and export deflection: Evidence from Iran. *Economic Policy, 32*(90), 319–355.

Hall, C. M. (1992). *Hallmark tourist events*. London: Belhaven Press.

Hall, C. M. (1994a). *Tourism and politics: Policy, power and place*. Chichester: John Wiley & Sons.

Hall, C. M. (1994b). *Tourism in the Pacific Rim*. London: Belhaven.

Hall, C. M. (2002). Travel safety, terrorism and the media: The significance of the issue-attention cycle. *Current Issues in Tourism, 5*(5), 458–466.

Hall, C. M. (2005). *Tourism: Rethinking the social science of mobility*. Harlow: Pearson.

Hall, C. M. (2008). *Tourism planning: Policies, processes and relationships* (2nd edn.). Harlow: Pearson Education.

Hall, C. M. (2012). Sustainable mega-events: Beyond the myth of balanced approaches to mega-event sustainability. *Event Management, 16*(2), 119–131.

Hall, C. M. (2013). Tourism, visas and the geopolitics of mobility: "We are all terror suspects now". In B. Lovelock & K. Lovelock (Eds.), *The ethics of tourism-critical and applied perspectives* (pp. 53–58). Abingdon: Routledge.

Hall, C. M. (2016). Intervening in academic interventions: Framing social marketing's potential for successful sustainable tourism behavioural change. *Journal of Sustainable Tourism, 24*(3), 350–375.

Hall, C. M. (2017). Tourism and geopolitics: The political imaginary of territory, tourism and space. In D. Hall (Ed.), *Tourism and geopolitics: Issues from Central and Eastern Europe* (pp. 15–24). Wallingford: CABI.

Hall, C. M., & O'Sullivan, V. (1996). Tourism, political stability and violence. In A. Pizam & Y. Mansfeld (Eds.), *Tourism, crime and international security issues* (pp. 105–121). Chichester: John Wiley & Sons.

Hall, C. M., Prayag, G., & Amore, A. (2017). *Tourism and resilience: Individual, organisational and destination perspectives*. Bristol: Channel View Publications.

Hall, C. M., & Ringer, G. (2000). Tourism in Cambodia, Laos and Myanmar: From terrorism to tourism. In C. M. Hall & S. J. Page (Eds.), *Tourism in South and South-East Asia: Critical perspectives* (pp. 178–194). Oxford: Butterworth-Heinemann.

Hall, C. M., Timothy, D. J., & Duval, D. T. (2004). Security and tourism: Towards a new understanding? *Journal of Travel & Tourism Marketing, 15*(2–3), 1–18.

Hall, D. (Ed.). (2017). *Tourism and geopolitics: Issues and concepts from central and eastern Europe.* Wallingford: CABI.

Halliday, D. J. (1999). Iraq and the UN's weapon of mass destruction. *Current History, 98*(625), 65–68.

Hanlon, J., & Omond, R. (1987). *The sanctions handbook.* Harmondsworth: Penguin Books.

Hannam, K., Butler, G., & Paris, C. M. (2014). Developments and key issues in tourism mobilities. *Annals of Tourism Research, 44*, 171–185.

Happold, M., & Eden, P. (Eds.). (2019). *Economic sanctions and international law.* London: Bloomsbury Publishing.

Harrus, F. (2015). Le tourisme turc victime des représailles russes [Turkish tourism victim of Russian retaliation]. Retrieved from www.francetvinfo.fr/monde/russie/le-tourisme-turc-victime-des-represailles-russes_3066431.html

Hazbun, W. (2004). Globalisation, reterritorialisation and the political economy of tourism development in the Middle East. *Geopolitics, 9*(2), 310–341.

Hellquist, E. (2018). Ostracism and the EU's contradictory approach to sanctions at home and abroad. *Contemporary Politics.* https://doi.org/10.1080/13569775.2018.1553083

Helms, J. (1999). What sanctions epidemic? US business' curious crusade. *Foreign Affairs, 78*(1), 2–8.

Henderson, J. C. (2003). The politics of tourism in Myanmar. *Current Issues in Tourism, 6*(2), 97–118.

Henderson, J. C. (2007). *Tourism crises: Causes, consequences and management.* London: Elsevier.

Hitchcock, J. (2016). Social media rhetoric of the transnational Palestinian-led boycott, divestment, and sanctions movement. *Social Media+ Society, 2*(1). doi:10.1177/2056305116634367

Ho, E. L.-E. (2013). "Refugee" or "returnee"? The ethnic geopolitics of diasporic resettlement in China and intergenerational change. *Transactions of the Institute of British Geographers, 38*(4), 599–611.

Hoikkala, H., & Magnusson, N. (2019). As "flying shame" grips Sweden, SAS ups stakes in climate battle. *Bloomberg*, 14 April. Retrieved from www.bloomberg.com/news/articles/2019-04-14/as-flying-shame-grips-sweden-sas-ups-stakes-in-climate-battle

Holmes, O. (2019). Rashida Tlaib rejects Israel's offer for "humanitarian" visit to West Bank. *The Guardian*, 16 August. Retrieved from www.theguardian.com/us-news/2019/aug/16/israel-to-allow-entry-to-rashida-tlaib-for-humanitarian-visit

Howard, P. H., & Allen, P. (2010). Beyond organic and fair trade? An analysis of ecolabel preferences in the United States. *Rural Sociology, 75*(2), 244–269.

Hoyle, B. (2007). Muslim world inflamed by Rushdie knighthood. *Times Online*, 19 June. Retrieved from www.thetimes.co.uk/article/muslim-world-inflamed-by-rushdie-knighthood-hbgq2r6wmlv

Hudson, S. (2007). To go or not to go? Ethical perspectives on tourism in an "outpost of tyranny". *Journal of Business Ethics, 76*(4), 385–396.

Hudson, S. (2016). Let the journey begin (again): The branding of Myanmar. *Journal of Destination Marketing & Management, 5*(4), 305–313.

Hufbauer, G. (1998). Economic sanctions. *Proceedings of the ASIL Annual Meeting, 92*, 332–335.

Hufbauer, G. C., & Oegg, B. (2000). *Targeted sanctions: A policy alternative.* Paper prepared for Symposium on "Sanctions Reform? Evaluating the Economic Weapon in Asia and the World." 23 February. Retrieved from www.piie.com/commentary/speeches-papers/targeted-sanctions-policy-alternative

Hufbauer, G. C., & Oegg, B. (2003). Beyond the nation-state: Privatization of economic sanctions. *Middle East Policy, 10*(2), 126–134.

Hufbauer, G. C., Schott, J. J., & Elliott, K. A. (1990). *Economic sanctions reconsidered: History and current policy* (2nd edn.). Washington, DC: Institute for International Economics.

Hufbauer, G. C., Schott, J. J., Elliott, K. A., & Oeggm, B. (2008). *Economic sanctions reconsidered* (3rd edn.). Washington, DC: The Peterson Institute for International Economics.

Hughes, C. W. (2006). The political economy of Japanese sanctions towards North Korea: Domestic coalitions and international systemic pressures. *Pacific Affairs, 79*(3), 455–481.

Humane Research Council. (2008). Animal tracker-wave 1. Retrieved from http://big.assets.huffingtonpost.com/hrcpoll.pdf

Hyman, P. E. (1980). Immigrant women and consumer protest: The New York City kosher meat boycott of 1902. *American Jewish History, 70*(1), 91.

Inglehart, R., Haerpfer, C., Moreno, A., Welzel, C., Kizilova, K., Diez-Medrano, J., . . . Puranen, B. (Eds.). (2014). *World values survey: All rounds: Country-pooled datafile version.* Madrid: JD Systems Institute. Retrieved from www.worldvaluessurvey.org/WVSDocumentationWVL.jsp

Iran Daily. (2018). Minister proposes Persian language be taught at Russian schools. Retrieved from http://iran-daily.com/News/213518.html

Irving, S., Harrison, R., & Rayner, M. (2002). Ethical consumerism: Democracy through the wallet. *Journal of Research for Consumers, 3*(3), 63–83.

Isaac, R. K., Hall, C. M., & Higgins-Desbiolles, F. (Eds.). (2015). *The politics and power of tourism in Palestine.* Abingdon: Routledge.

Ivanov, S., Sypchenko, L., & Webster, C. (2017). International sanctions and Russia's hotel industry: The impact on business and coping mechanisms of hoteliers. *Tourism Planning & Development, 14*(3), 430–441.

Jaeger, M. D. (2018). *Coercive sanctions and international conflicts: A sociological theory.* Abingdon: Routledge.

Jalili, S. (2019). Iran stops stamping passports. *Al-Monitor.* Retrieved from www.al-monitor.com/pulse/originals/2019/06/iran-stops-stamping-passports.html

Jeong, J. M., & Peksen, D. (2019). Domestic institutional constraints, veto players, and sanction effectiveness. *Journal of Conflict Resolution, 63*(1), 194–217.

John, A., & Klein, J. (2003). The boycott puzzle: Consumer motivations for purchase sacrifice. *Management Science, 49*(9), 1196–1209.

Joyner, C. C. (2018). Sanctions and international law. In D. Cortright & G. A. Lopez (Eds.), *Economic sanctions: Panacea or peacebuilding in a post-cold war world?* (pp. 73–87). Abingdon: Routledge.

Kaempfer, W. H., & Lowenberg, A. D. (2007). The political economy of economic sanctions. In T. Sandler & K. Hartley (Eds.), *Handbook of defense economics: Defense in a globalized world* (Vol. 2, pp. 867–911). Amsterdam: North-Holland.

Kelm, O., & Dohle, M. (2018). Information, communication and political consumerism: How (online) information and (online) communication influence boycotts and buycotts. *New Media & Society, 20*(4), 1523–1542.

Kemp, S. (2017). Heritage and the meaning of "development" in Myanmar. *Historic Environment, 29*(3), 44.

Kendrick, A., Fullerton, J. A., & Broyles, S. J. (2015). Would I go? US citizens react to a Cuban tourism campaign. *Place Branding and Public Diplomacy, 11*(4), 249–262.

Keys, B. (2018). Harnessing human rights to the Olympic Games: Human Rights Watch and the 1993 "Stop Beijing" campaign. *Journal of Contemporary History, 53*(2), 415–438.

Khodadadi, M. (2016a). A new dawn? The Iran nuclear deal and the future of the Iranian tourism industry. *Tourism Management Perspectives, 18*, 6–9.

Khodadadi, M. (2016b). Return to glory? Prospects of Iran's hospitality sector post-nuclear deal. *Tourism Management Perspectives, 19*, 16–18.

Kilani, S. E. (2003). Boycott fever in Jordan. *Middle East Report, 226*, 24–27.

Kim, H. S. (2018). When public diplomacy faces trade barriers and diplomatic frictions: The case of the Korean Wave. *Place Branding and Public Diplomacy, 14*(4), 234–244.

King, B. G. (2008a). A political mediation model of corporate response to social movement activism. *Administrative Science Quarterly, 53*, 395–421.

King, B. G. (2008b). A social movement perspective of stakeholder collective action and influence. *Business & Society, 47*, 21–49.

Kinnear, T. C., Taylor, J. R., & Ahmed, S. A. (1974). Ecologically concerned consumers: Who are they? Ecologically concerned consumers can be identified. *Journal of Marketing, 38*(2), 20–24.

Klein, J. G., Smith, N. C., & John, A. (2004). Why we boycott: Consumer motivations for boycott participation. *Journal of Marketing, 68*(3), 92–109.

Kline, J. M. (1999). Continuing controversies over state and local foreign policy sanctions in the United States. *Publius: The Journal of Federalism, 29*(2), 111–134.

Klooster, D. (2005). Environmental certification of forests: The evolution of environmental governance in a commodity network. *Journal of Rural Studies, 21*(4), 403–417.

Knight, J. G., Mitchell, B. S., & Gao, H. (2009). Riding out the Muhammad cartoons crisis: Contrasting strategies and outcomes. *Long Range Planning, 42*(1), 6–22.

Koch, S. (2015). A typology of political conditionality beyond aid: Conceptual horizons based on lessons from the European Union. *World Development, 75*, 98–108.

Koku, P. (2012). On the effectiveness of consumer boycotts organized through the internet: The market model. *Journal of Services Marketing, 26*(1), 20–26.

Korhonen, I., Simola, H., & Solanko, L. (2018). Sanctions and countersanctions: Effects on economy, trade and finance. *Focus on European Economic Integration, Oesterreichische Nationalbank (Austrian Central Bank), Q3*(18), 68–76.

Kozinets, R. V., & Handelman, J. (1998). Ensouling consumption: A netnographic exploration of the meaning of boycotting behavior. In J.W. Alba & W. Hutchinson (Eds), Advances in Consumer Research (pp. 475–480). Provo, UT: Association for Consumer Research.

Krain, M. (2017). The effect of economic sanctions on the severity of genocides or politicides. *Journal of Genocide Research, 19*(1), 88–111.

Krauss, C. (2019). New U.S. sanctions on Venezuela aim to choke off government's finances. *New York Times*. Retrieved from www.nytimes.com/2019/04/17/business/us-venezuela-sanctions-maduro.html

Kreutz, J. (2015). Human rights, geostrategy, and EU foreign policy, 1989–2008. *International Organization, 69*(1), 195–217.

Kunz, J. L. (1960). Sanctions in international law. *American Journal of International Law, 54*(2), 324–347.

Kustra, T. (2018). Sanctioning the homeland: Diasporas' influence on American economic sanctions policy, 6 August. Retrieved from https://ssrn.com/abstract=3227090 or http://dx.doi.org/10.2139/ssrn.3227090

Laidler, H. W. (1913). *Boycotts and the labor struggle*. New York: Russell and Russell.

Lavy, V. (1984). The economic embargo of Egypt by Arab states: Myth and reality. *Middle East Journal, 38*(3), 419–432.

Lektzian, D., & Souva, M. (2003). The economic peace between democracies: Economic sanctions and domestic institutions. *Journal of Peace Research, 40*(6), 641–660.

Le Monde. (2018). Avec le retrait de l'accord sur le nucléaire, l'économie iranienne se prépare au pire [With the withdrawal of the nuclear deal, the Iranian economy is preparing for the worst]. Retrieved from www.lemonde.fr/economie/article/2018/05/09/avec-le-retrait-des-etats-unis-de-l-accord-sur-le-nucleaire-l-economie-iranienne-se-prepare-au-pire_5296524_3234.html

Lempkowicz, Y. (2019). Israel rejects Amnesty International's call to boycott Israeli tourism sites in Judea and Samaria. *EJP European Jewish Press*, 30 January. Retrieved from https://ejpress.org/israel-rejects-amnesty-internationals-call-to-boycott-israeli-tourism-sites-in-judea-and-samaria/

Leogrande, W. M. (1996). Making the economy scream: US economic sanctions against Sandinista Nicaragua. *Third World Quarterly, 17*(2), 329–348.

Leonidou, L. C., Leonidou, C. N., & Kvasova, O. (2010). Antecedents and outcomes of consumer environmentally friendly attitudes and behaviour. *Journal of Marketing Management, 26*(13–14), 1319–1344.

L'Etang, J., Falkheimer, J., & Lugo, J. (2007). Public relations and tourism: Critical reflections and a research agenda. *Public Relations Review, 33*(1), 68–76.

Lilljegren, J. (2016). Euskadi-bulletinen: Swedish solidarity with the Basque Independence Movement during the 1970's. *BOGA: Basque Studies Consortium Journal, 4*(1), 3.

Listhaug, O., & Grønflaten, L. (2007). Civic decline? Trends in political involvement and participation in Norway, 1965–2001. *Scandinavian Political Studies, 30*(2), 272–299.

Loader, B. D., Vromen, A., & Xenos, M. A. (2014). The networked young citizen: Social media, political participation and civic engagement. *Information, Communication & Society*, *17*(2), 143–150.

Lopez, G. A., & Cortright, D. (2018). Economic sanctions in contemporary global relations. In D. Cortright & G. A. Lopez (Eds.), *Economic sanctions: Panacea or peacebuilding in a post-cold war world?* (pp. 3–16). Abingdon: Routledge.

Losman, D. L. (1972). The Arab boycott of Israel. *International Journal of Middle East Studies*, *3*(2), 99–122.

Lovelock, B. (2012). Human rights and human travel? Modeling global travel patterns under an ethical tourism regime. *Tourism Review International*, *16*(3–4), 183–202.

Luo, Q., & Zhai, X. (2017). "I will never go to Hong Kong again!" How the secondary crisis communication of "Occupy Central" on Weibo shifted to a tourism boycott. *Tourism Management*, *62*, 159–172.

Macaulay, J. (2007). Tourism and the transformation of Cuba-revisited. *Cornell Hotel and Restaurant Administration Quarterly*, *48*(4), 419–422.

MacDonald, R. A., & McDonald, K. (2014). Case study: Tragic kingdom? The Southern Baptist Convention boycott of Walt Disney. *Christian Business Academy Review*, *9*. Retrieved from https://cbfa-cbar.org/index.php/cbar/article/view/31

Mack, A., & Khan, A. (2000). The efficacy of UN sanctions. *Security Dialogue*, *31*(3), 279–292.

MacQueen, K. (2005). From sea to stinking sea. *Macleans*, 17 October. Retrieved from www.macleans.ca/topstories/canada/article.jsp?content=20051017_113470_113470

Mahoney, J. (1976). The relation of anticipated effectiveness, alienation, and values structure to planned participation in a national meat boycott. *Psychology*, *13*(2), 39–47.

Makarem, S. C., & Jae, H. (2016). Consumer boycott behavior: An exploratory analysis of twitter feeds. *Journal of Consumer Affairs*, *50*(1), 193–223.

Makortoff, K. (2019). Standard Chartered fined $1.1bn for money-laundering and sanctions breaches. *The Guardian*. Retrieved from www.theguardian.com/business/2019/apr/09/standard-chartered-fined-money-laundering-sanctions-breaches

Maller, T. (2010). Diplomacy derailed: The consequences of diplomatic sanctions. *The Washington Quarterly*, *33*(3), 61–79.

María, G. A., Mazas, B., Zarza, F. J., & de la Lama, G. C. M. (2017). Animal welfare, National Identity and social change: attitudes and opinions of Spanish citizens towards bullfighting. *Journal of Agricultural and Environmental Ethics*, 30(6), 809–826.

Masters, J. (2019). What are economic sanctions? *Council on Foreign Relations*. Retrieved from www.cfr.org/backgrounder/what-are-economic-sanctions

Matelly, S, Gomez, C., & Carcanague, S. (2017). Performance des sanctions internationals [performance of international sanctions]. Retrieved from www.iris-france.org/wp-content/uploads/2017/06/rapport_final_persan_juin_2017_0.pdf

McCormick, E. (2019). "Boycott Iowa": Latest twist in legal tussle between animal campaigners and US farmers. *The Guardian*, 16 March. Retrieved from www.theguardian.com/environment/2019/mar/16/boycott-iowa-latest-twist-in-legal-tussle-between-animal-campaigners-and-us-farmers

McDonnell, M. H., & King, B. (2013). Keeping up appearances: Reputational threat and impression management after social movement boycotts. *Administrative Science Quarterly*, *58*(3), 387–419.

McDonnell, P. (2010). Hotel workers accuse LAX Hilton of circumventing L.A.'s "living wage" law. *Los Angeles Times*, 17 June. Retrieved from www.latimes.com/archives/la-xpm-2010-jun-17-la-me-hilton-20100617-story.html

McGriff, J. A. (2012). A conceptual topic in marketing management: The emerging need for protecting and managing brand equity: The case of online consumer brand boycotts. *International Management Review*, *8*(1), 49–54.

McLaughlin, K. (2004). Is your grocery list politically correct? Retrieved from www.wsj.com/articles/SB107698348237931093

McLean, E. V., & Whang, T. (2014). Designing foreign policy: Voters, special interest groups, and economic sanctions. *Journal of Peace Research*, *51*(5), 589–602.

Mehmet, M., & Simmons, P. (2019). Operationalizing social media in upstream social marketing. *Journal of Social Marketing*, *9*(3), 288–308.

Mercille, J. (2008). The radical geopolitics of US foreign policy: Geopolitical and geoeconomic logics of power. *Political Geography*, *27*(5), 570–586.

Micheletti, M., & Stolle, D. (2008). Fashioning social justice through political consumerism, capitalism, and the internet. *Cultural Studies*, *22*(5), 749–769.

Middle East Eye. (2017). Qatar tourism sector starts to feel squeeze of blockade: Hotels recorded lower-than-expected visitor numbers over the Eid festival on Sunday. *Reuters*, 27 June. Retrieved from www.middleeasteye.net/news/qatar-tourism-sector-starts-feel-squeeze-blockade

Middle East Monitor (MEM). (2019). Amnesty calls for travel companies to boycott Israel settlements. Retrieved from www.middleeastmonitor.com/20190130-amnesty-calls-for-travel-companies-to-boycott-israel-settlements/

Miller, T. (2016). Greenwashed sports and environmental activism: Formula 1 and FIFA. *Environmental Communication*, *10*(6), 719–733.

Miller, V. (2017). Phatic culture and the status quo: Reconsidering the purpose of social media activism. *Convergence*, *23*(3), 251–269.

Mills, C. W. (1994). Revisionist ontologies: Theorizing white supremacy. *Social and Economic Studies*, *43*(3), 105–134.

Morello, L., & Reardon, S. (2017). Meet the scientists affected by Trump's immigration ban. *Nature News*, *542*(7639), 13.

Moret, E. S. (2015). Humanitarian impacts of economic sanctions on Iran and Syria. *European Security*, *24*(1), 120–140.

Morgan, T. C., & Schwebach, V. L. (1997). Fools suffer gladly: The use of economic sanctions in international crises. *International Studies Quarterly*, *41*(1), 27–50.

The Moscow Times. (2019). Russian flight ban could cost Georgia $300M, experts say. 24 June. Retrieved from www.themoscowtimes.com/2019/06/24/russian-flight-ban-could-cost-georgia-300m-experts-say-a66132

Motamedi, M. (2019). Iran wants more Chinese tourists: A whole lot more. *Aljazeera*. Retrieved from www.aljazeera.com/ajimpact/iran-chinese-tourists-lot-190806192455555.html

Mueller, J., & Mueller, K. (1999). Sanctions of mass destruction. *Foreign Affairs, 78*(3), 43–53.

Mulligan, S. (2018). *The United States and the "world court"*. Washington, DC: Congressional Research Service.

Nafziger, J. A. R. (1980). Diplomatic fun and the games: A commentary on the United States boycott of the 1980 Summer Olympics. *Willamette Law Review, 17*, 67–81.

Naylor, R. T. (2001). *Economic warfare: Sanctions, embargo busting, and their human cost*. Boston, MA: Northeastern University Press.

Neumayer, E. (2006). Unequal access to foreign spaces: How states use visa restrictions to regulate mobility in a globalized world. *Transactions of the Institute of British Geographers, 31*(1), 72–84.

Nguyen, T., Ngo, H., Ngo, P., & Kang, G. D. (2018). Understanding the motivations influencing ecological boycott participation: An exploratory study in Viet Nam. *Sustainability, 10*(12), 4786.

Nicholson, M. (1967). Tariff wars and a model of conflict. *Journal of Peace Research, 4*(1), 26–38.

Nielsen, H., & Gibbon, P. (2011). *Pro-poor growth through export sector support: What works where and why?* DIIS Report No. 2011: 15. Copenhagen: Danish Institute for International Studies.

Nossal, K. R. (1989). International sanctions as international punishment. *International Organization, 43*(2), 301–322.

Novoderezhkin, A. (2015). Major Russian operator suspends sales of packages to Turkey. *Tass*, 25 November. Retrieved from https://tass.com/politics/838873

Office of Foreign Assets Control (OFAC). (2019). OFAC research center, sanctions programs and country information. Retrieved from www.treasury.gov/resource-center/sanctions/Programs/Pages/Programs.aspx

Oliphant, R. (2015). Russia "considering exit visas" for citizens travelling abroad. *The Telegraph*, 13 November. Retrieved from www.telegraph.co.uk/news/worldnews/europe/russia/11994915/Russia-considering-exit-visas-for-citizens-travelling-abroad.html

Olson, E. D., & Park, H. (2018). The impact of religious freedom laws on destination image. *Cornell Hospitality Quarterly*. doi:1938965518815659

Oltermann, P. (2019). German parliament declares Israel boycott campaign antisemitic. *The Guardian*, 17 May. Retrieved from www.theguardian.com/world/2019/may/17/german-parliament-declares-israel-boycott-campaign-antisemitic

Oppmann, P., & Vazquez, M. (2019). Trump admin imposes new travel restrictions on Cuba, banning cruise ships. *CNN*, 4 June. Retrieved from https://edition.cnn.com/2019/06/04/politics/us-cuba-travel-restrictions/index.html

O'Sullivan, M. L. (2010). Iran and the great sanctions debate. *The Washington Quarterly, 33*(4), 7–21.

Ovcharov, A. O., Ismagilova, G. N., Ziganshin, I. I., & Rysayeva, M. A. (2015). The influence of Western countries' sanctions on the development of the Russian exit tourism. *Asian Social Sciences, 11*(11), 289–296.

Pacelle, W. (1993). The evolution of wildlife management ethics: From human-centred to humane. *George Wright Forum, 10*(2), 45–52.

Pape, R. A. (1997). Why economic sanctions do not work. *International Security, 22*(2), 90–136.

Parsons, E. C. M. (2003). Seal management in Scotland: Tourist perceptions and the possible impacts on the Scottish tourism industry. *Current Issues in Tourism, 6*, 540–546.

Parsons, E. C. M., & Rawles, C. (2003). The resumption of whaling by Iceland and the potential negative impact in the Icelandic whale-watching market. *Current Issues in Tourism, 6*(5), 444–448.

Pedersen, M. B. (2013). How to promote human rights in the world's most repressive states: Lessons from Myanmar. *Australian Journal of International Affairs, 67*(2), 190–202.

Peksen, D. (2009). Better or worse? The effect of economic sanctions on human rights. *Journal of Peace Research, 46*(1), 59–77.

Perlez, J., Huang, Y., & Mozur, P. (2017). How North Korea managed to defy years of sanctions. *The New York Times*. Retrieved from www.nytimes.com/2017/05/12/world/asia/north-korea-sanctions-loopholes-china-united-states-garment-industry.html

Pezzullo, P. C. (2011). Contextualizing boycotts and buycotts: The impure politics of consumer-based advocacy in an age of global ecological crises. *Communication and Critical/Cultural Studies, 8*(2), 124–145.

Phillips, D. (2019). Corporations pile pressure on Brazil over Amazon fires. *The Guardian*, 30 August. Retrieved from www.theguardian.com/world/2019/aug/30/corporations-pile-pressure-on-brazil-over-amazon-fires-crisis

Philp, J., & Mercer, D. (1999). Commodification of Buddhism in contemporary Burma. *Annals of Tourism Research, 26*(1), 21–54.

Pile, T. (2018). Tourism boycotts: Why people gave Myanmar a miss and skipped South Korea? And what about plucky little Palau? Retrieved from www.scmp.com/magazines/post-magazine/travel/article/2165997/tourism-boycotts-why-people-gave-myanmar-miss-and

Pirie, G. H. (1990). Aviation, apartheid and sanctions: Air transport to and from South Africa, 1945–1989. *GeoJournal, 22*(3), 231–240.

Popesku, J., & Hall, D. R. (2004). Sustainability as the basis for future tourism development in Serbia. In D. R. Hall (Ed.), *Tourism and transition: Governance, transformation and development* (pp. 95–103). Wallingford: CABI.

Portela, C. (2010). *European Union sanctions and foreign policy: When and why do they work*. Abingdon: Routledge.

Portela, C. (2016). Are European Union sanctions "targeted"? *Cambridge Review of International Affairs, 29*(3), 912–929.

Porter, R. C. (1979). International trade and investment sanctions: Potential impact on the South African economy. *Journal of Conflict Resolution, 23*(4), 579–612.

Power, M., & Campbell, D. (2010). The state of critical geopolitics. *Political Geography, 29*(5), 243–246.

Pratt, S., & Alizadeh, V. (2018). The economic impact of the lifting of sanctions on tourism in Iran: A computable general equilibrium analysis. *Current Issues in Tourism, 21*(11), 1221–1238.

Pritchard, A., Morgan, N. J., Sedgley, D., Khan, E., & Jenkins, A. (2000). Sexuality and holiday choices: Conversations with gay and lesbian tourists. *Leisure Studies*, *19*(4), 267–282.

Puar, J. K. (2002). Circuits of queer mobility: Tourism, travel and globalization. *GLQ*, *8*, 101–138.

Quandt, W. B. (2016). *Camp David: Peacemaking and politics*. Washington, DC: Brookings Institution Press.

Ram, Y., Kama, A., Isaac, M., & Hall, C. M. (2019). The benefits of an LGBT inclusive tourist destination. *Journal of Destination Marketing & Management*. doi:10.1016/j.jdmm.2019.100374

Reardon, S. (2017). How the latest US travel ban could affect science. *Nature News*, *550*(7674), 17.

Regelin, W. L., Valkenburg, P., & Boertje, R. D. (2005). Management of large predators in Alaska. *Wildlife Biology in Practice*, *1*(1), 77–85.

Reiser, D. (2003). Globalisation: An old phenomenon that needs to be rediscovered for tourism? *Tourism and Hospitality Research*, *4*(4), 306–320.

Reisman, W. M., & Stevick, D. L. (1998). The applicability of international law standards to United Nations economic sanctions programmes. *European Journal of International Law*, *9*(1), 86–141.

Reith, S., & Nauright, J. (2005). Ethics, economics and tourism: Myanmar as a case study. *Tourism Recreation Research*, *30*(2), 81–85.

Reuters. (2019). Brunei says it will not enforce gay sex death penalty after backlash. *The Guardian*, 5 May. Retrieved from www.theguardian.com/world/2019/may/05/brunei-says-it-will-not-enforce-lgbt-gay-sex-death-penalty-after-backlash

Reuters in Beijing. (2019). China vows to impose sanctions on US firms supplying Taiwan military. *The Guardian*, 12 July. Retrieved from www.theguardian.com/world/2019/jul/12/china-taiwan-sanctions-us-firms-military-sales

Richards, J. (2019). Boycott companies that are inhumane and cruel to animals. Retrieved from www.humanedecisions.com/boycott-companies-that-are-inhumane-and-cruel-to-animals/

Richardson, M. (2005). Australia-Southeast Asia relations and the East Asian summit. *Australian Journal of International Affairs*, *59*(3), 351–365.

Robison, S. (2014). No end to caring? Politics and the moral riptide of human evolution. *Politics and the Life Sciences*, *33*(1), 2–32.

Rogoff, K. (2015). Economic sanctions have a long and chequered history. *The Guardian*, 5 January. Retrieved from www.theguardian.com/business/2015/jan/05/economic-sanctions-long-history-mixed-success

Rollin, B. E. (2011). Animal rights as a mainstream phenomenon. *Animals*, *1*(1), 102–115.

Rosencranz, A. (1986). The acid rain controversy in Europe and North America: A political analysis. *Ambio*, *15*(1), 47–51.

Roser-Renouf, C., Atkinson, L., Maibach, E., & Leiserowitz, A. (2016). The consumer as climate activist. *International Journal of Communication*, *10*, 4759–4783.

Rossignol, M. (1996). *Sanctions, the economic weapon in the new world order* (Rev. edn.). Library of Parliament BP-346E. Ottawa: Research Branch, Political and Social Affairs Division, Library of Parliament, Government of Canada.

Rowat, C. (2014). Explainer: Do sanctions work? *The Conversation*. Retrieved from https://theconversation.com/explainer-do-sanctions-work-24431

Ruijgrok, K. (2017). From the web to the streets: Internet and protests under authoritarian regimes. *Democratization*, *24*(3), 498–520.

Sæþórsdóttir, A. D., & Hall, C. M. (2019). Contested development paths and rural communities: Sustainable energy or sustainable tourism in Iceland? *Sustainability*, *11*, 3642.

Sæþórsdóttir, A. D., Hall, C. M., & Stefánsson, Þ. (2019). Senses by seasons: Tourists' perceptions depending on seasonality in popular nature destinations in Iceland. *Sustainability*, *11*, 3059.

Safaeian, B. (2019). Iran is offering itself as cheaper destination for medical tourism. *Iran Trawell*. Retrieved from https://en.irantrawell.com/iran-is-offering-itself-as-cheaper-destination-for-medical-tourism/

Şahin, E., Konak, F., & Karaca, S. S. (2017). Impact of "aircraft crisis" between Turkey and Russia on Borsa Istanbul food, beverage and tourism indexes. *Business and Economics Research Journal*, *8*(3), 473–485.

Saldanha, A. (2002). Identity, spatiality and post-colonial resistance: Geographies of the tourism critique in Goa. *Current Issues in Tourism*, *5*(2), 92–111.

Sapontzis, S. (Ed.). (2004). *Food for thought: The debate over eating meat*. Amherst, MA: Prometheus Books.

Saunders, P. L. (2014). When sanctions led to war. *New York Times*, 21 August. Retrieved from www.nytimes.com/2014/08/22/opinion/when-sanctions-lead-to-war.html

Schreiber, E. (2018). Tunisia could lose chance to host World Chess meet after banning Israelis. *The Jerusalem Post*, 29 July. Retrieved from www.jpost.com/Arab-Israeli-Conflict/Tunisia-could-lose-chance-to-host-World-Chess-meet-after-banning-Israelis-563689

Sedelmeier, U. (2017). Political safeguards against democratic backsliding in the EU: The limits of material sanctions and the scope of social pressure. *Journal of European Public Policy*, *24*(3), 337–351.

Selden, Z. A. (1999). *Economic sanctions as instruments of American foreign policy*. Westport, CN: Praeger.

Selser, G. (2019). EU hits Nicaragua on rights, seeks sanctions as talks resume. *Bloomberg*, 15 March. Retrieved from www.bloomberg.com/news/articles/2019-03-14/eu-hits-nicaragua-on-rights-seeks-sanctions-as-talks-resume

Sen, S., Gürhan-Canli, Z., & Morwitz, V. (2001). Withholding consumption: A social dilemma perspective on consumer boycotts. *Journal of Consumer Research*, *28*(3), 399–417.

Sergie, M., & Odeh, L. (2018). Qatar's battered tourism sector will need three years to recover. *Bloomberg*, 10 October. Retrieved from www.bloomberg.com/news/articles/2018-10-10/qatar-s-battered-tourism-sector-will-need-three-years-to-recover

Servettaz, E. (2014). A sanctions primer: What happens to the targeted? *World Affairs*, *177*(2), 82–89.

Seyfi, S., & Hall, C. M. (Eds.). (2018a). *Tourism in Iran: Challenges, development and issues*. Abingdon: Routledge.

Seyfi, S., & Hall, C. M. (2018b). Tourism in Iran: An introduction. In S. Seyfi & C. M. Hall (Eds.). (2019), *Tourism in Iran: Challenges, development and issues*. Abingdon: Routledge.

Seyfi, S., & Hall, C. M. (2018c). The future(s) of tourism in Iran. In S. Seyfi & C. M. Hall (Eds.). (2019), *Tourism in Iran: Challenges, development and issues*. Abingdon: Routledge.

Seyfi, S., & Hall, C. M. (2019a). International sanctions, tourism destinations and resistive economy. *Journal of Policy Research in Tourism, Leisure and Events*, *11*(1), 159–169.

Seyfi, S., & Hall, C. M. (2019b). Sanctions and tourism: Effects, complexities and research. *Tourism Geographies*. doi:10.1080/14616688.2019.1663911

Seyfi, S., Hall, C. M., & Fagnoni, E. (2019). Managing World Heritage Site stakeholders: A grounded theory paradigm model approach. *Journal of Heritage Tourism*, *14*(4), 308–324.

Seyfi, S., Hall, C. M., & Kuhzady, S. (2019). Tourism and hospitality research on Iran: Current state and perspectives. *Tourism Geographies*, *21*(1), 143–162.

Shah, A. (2005). United States and the International Criminal Court. *Global Issues*, 25 September. Retrieved from www.globalissues.org/article/490/united-states-and-the-icc

Shah, D., McLeod, D., Kim, E., Lee, S. Y., Gotleib, M., Ho, S., & Brievik, H. (2007). Political consumerism: How communication and consumption orientations drive "lifestyle politics". *The Annals of the American Academy of Political and Social Science*, *611*(1), 217–235.

Shaheer, I., Carr, N., & Insch, A. (2019). What are the reasons behind tourism boycotts? *Anatolia*, 1–3.

Shaheer, I., Insch, A., & Carr, N. (2018). Tourism destination boycotts: Are they becoming a standard practise? *Tourism Recreation Research*, *43*(1), 129–132.

Sherwood, H., & Kalman, M. (2013). Stephen Hawking joins academic boycott of Israel. *The Guardian*, 8 May. Retrieved from www.theguardian.com/world/2013/may/08/stephen-hawking-israel-academic-boycott

Simons, G. L. (1999). *Imposing economic sanctions: Legal remedy or genocidal tool?* London: Pluto Press.

Singleton, B. E. (2018). Making a meal of it: A political ecology examination of whale meat and tourism. In C. Kline (Eds.), *Tourism experiences and animal consumption: Contested values, morality and ethics* (pp. 87–101). Abingdon: Routledge.

Skjærseth, J. B., & Skodvin, T. (2001). Climate change and the oil industry: Common problems, different strategies. *Global Environmental Politics*, *1*(4), 43–64.

Sleigh, S. (2019). TfL Tube chiefs ban adverts from 11 countries over poor human rights. *Evening Standard*, 2 May. Retrieved from www.standard.co.uk/news/london/tube-chiefs-ban-adverts-from-11-countries-over-poor-human-rights-a4132321.html

Smeets, M. (2019). The theory and practice of economic sanctions. In S. Sutyrin, O. Y. Trofimenko, & A. Koval (Eds.), *Russian trade policy: Achievements, challenges and prospects* (pp. 66–78). Abingdon: Routledge.

Smith, N. C. (1990). *Morality and the market: Consumer pressure for corporate accountability.* London: Routledge.

Smyth, G. (2016). Deciphering the Iranian leader's call for a "resistance economy". *The Guardian*, 19 April. Retrieved from www.theguardian.com/world/iran-blog/2016/apr/19/iran-resistance-economy-tehranbureau

Sofka, J. R. (1997). The Jeffersonian idea of national security: Commerce, the Atlantic balance of power, and the Barbary war, 1786–1805. *Diplomatic History, 21*(4), 519–544.

Sreberny, A., & Gholami, R. (2016). *Iranian communities in Britain.* London: London Middle East Institute, SOAS, University of London. Retrieved from www.soas.ac.uk/lmei-cis/events/file113142.pdf

Steen, R. (2012). John Carlos: A salutary lesson in the power of sport. *The Independent*, 20 May. Retrieved from www.independent.co.uk/news/people/profiles/john-carlos-a-salutary-lesson-in-the-power-of-sport-7768760.html

Stolle, D., Hooghe, M., & Micheletti, M. (2005). Politics in the supermarket: Political consumerism as a form of political participation. *International Political Science Review, 26*(3), 245–269.

Suroor, H. (2012). Jallikattu: Irish group calls for tourism boycott. Retrieved from www.thehindu.com/news/international/Jallikattu-Irish-group-calls-for-tourism-boycott/article13379538.ece

Sykes, H. (2016). Olympic homonationalisms. *Public, 27*(53), 140–148.

Tabak, L., & Avraham, E. (2018). Country image repair strategies during an asymmetrical conflict: An analysis of the Gaza conflict in 2014. *International Journal of Strategic Communication, 12*(3), 237–251.

Tajuddin, A. (2018). Statelessness and ethnic cleansing of the Rohingyas in Myanmar: Time for serious international intervention. *Journal of Asia Pacific Studies, 4*(4), 422–450.

Takeyh, R., & Maloney, S. (2011). The self-limiting success of Iran sanctions. *International Affairs, 87*(6), 1297–1312.

Taylor, B. (2012). *Sanctions as grand strategy.* Abingdon: Routledge.

Taylor, M. (2017). The Trump travel ban's impact on tourism. *Travel Pulse.* Retrieved from www.travelpulse.com/news/impacting-travel/the-trump-travel-ban-s-impact-on-tourism.html

Tehran Times. (2017). Iran seeks to broaden travel ties with East Asia. *Tehran Times*, 12 May. Retrieved from www.tehrantimes.com/news/414273/Iran-seeks-to-broaden-travel-ties-with-East-Asia

Teye, V. B., & Diffenderfer, P. (1988). The impact of a convention boycott on metropolitan Arizona. *Visions in Leisure and Business, 7*(2), Article 5. Retrieved from https://scholarworks.bgsu.edu/visions/vol7/iss2/5

Thomas, E. (2010). Sudan's 2010 elections: Victories, boycotts and the future of a peace deal. *Review of African Political Economy, 37*(125), 373–379.

Thrall, N. (2018). BDS: How a controversial non-violent movement has transformed the Israeli-Palestinian debate. *The Guardian*, 14 August. Retrieved from www.theguardian.com/news/2018/aug/14/bds-boycott-divestment-sanctions-movement-transformed-israeli-palestinian-debate

Tilikidou, I., Delistavrou, A., & Sarmaniotis, C. (2013). Intentions to boycott "unethical" hotels: A conjoint analysis. *Tourismos, 8*(3), 21–38.

Tisdall, S. (2018). Money wars: How sanctions and tariffs became Trump's big guns. *The Guardian,* 19 August. Retrieved from www.theguardian.com/us-news/2018/aug/19/trump-money-wars-economic-sanctions-trade-tariffs-backfiring

Tolkach, D. (2018). A view of Occupy Central impacts on Hong Kong tourism from the other side of the Great Firewall: A rejoinder to Luo & Zhai. *Tourism Management, 67,* 307–311.

Torabian, P., & Miller, M. C. (2017). Freedom of movement for all? Unpacking racialized travel experiences. *Current Issues in Tourism, 20*(9), 931–945.

Trenin, D. (2015). How effective are economic sanctions? *World Economic Forum.* Retrieved from www.weforum.org/agenda/2015/02/how-effective-are-economic-sanctions/

Tsygankov, A. P. (2002). The culture of economic security: National identity and politico-economic ideas in the post-Soviet world. *International Politics, 39*(2), 153–173.

Turck, N. (1976). The Arab boycott of Israel. *Foreign Affairs, 55*(2), 472–493.

Turak, N. (2018). US rejects International Court of Justice ruling on Iran, continuing its isolationist charge. *CNBC,* 5 October. Retrieved from www.cnbc.com/2018/10/05/us-rejects-international-court-of-justice-ruling-on-iran-continuing-its-isolationist-charge.html

Tutu, D. (2014). We need an apartheid-style boycott to save the planet. *The Guardian,* 10 April. Retrieved from www.theguardian.com/commentisfree/2014/apr/10/divest-fossil-fuels-climate-change-keystone-xl

United Nations Security Council (2001). *Resolution 1373* (2001). Retrieved from https://www.unodc.org/pdf/crime/terrorism/res_1373_english.pdf

United Nation Security Council. (2019). Sanctions. Retrieved from www.un.org/securitycouncil/sanctions/information

Van Rheenen, D. (2014). A skunk at the garden party: The Sochi Olympics, state-sponsored homophobia and prospects for human rights through mega sporting events. *Journal of Sport & Tourism, 19*(2), 127–144.

Waitt, G. (2001). The city as tourist spectacle. In D. Holmes (Ed.), *Virtual globalization: Virtual spaces/tourist spaces* (pp. 220–230). London: Routledge.

Wallensteen, P. (2000). *A century of economic sanctions: A field revisited.* Uppsala Peace Research Papers No. 1. Uppsala: Department of Peace and Conflict Research Uppsala University, Sweden.

Warren, L. M., & Antonopoulou, E. (1990). The conservation of loggerhead turtles in Zakynthos, Greece. *Oryx, 24*(1), 15–22.

Watson, B. (2015). Do boycotts really work? *The Guardian,* 6 January. Retrieved from www.theguardian.com/vital-signs/2015/jan/06/boycotts-shopping-protests-activists-consumers

Wearne, S. (2018). Tourism development and whaling—heritage as sustainable future. *Tourism Planning & Development, 15*(1), 89–95.

Weaver, D. B. (2010). Geopolitical dimensions of sustainable tourism. *Tourism Recreation Research, 35*(1), 47–53.

Webster, C., & Ivanov, S. (2017). The ideologies of national security and tourist visa restrictions. *International Journal of Tourism Policy*, 6(3/4), 171–190.

Webster, C., Yen, C., & Hji-Avgoustis, S. (2016). RFRA and the hospitality industry in Indiana: Political shocks and empirical impacts on Indianapolis' hospitality and tourism industry. *International Journal of Tourism Cities*, 2(3), 221–231.

Weiss, M. A. (2007). *Arab League boycott of Israel.* Washington, DC: Library of Congress, Congressional Research Service.

Weiss, T. G. (1999). Sanctions as a foreign policy tool: Weighing humanitarian impulses. *Journal of Peace Research*, 36(5), 499–509.

Williams, A. (2019). Berlin bans Iranian airline after EU slaps sanctions on Tehran. *Handelsblatt Today*, 21 January. Retrieved from www.handelsblatt.com/today/politics/mahan-air-berlin-bans-iranian-airline-after-eu-slaps-sanctions-on-tehran/23890736.html?ticket=ST-3083429-r0V7Xl0b6DNPOP33ufRp-ap3

Wilson, J., & Látková, P. (2016). American tourists in Cuba: Is the communist country a forbidden or a tainted fruit? *Tourism and Hospitality Research*, 16(1), 6–18.

Wolfsfeld, G., Segev, E., & Sheafer, T. (2013). Social media and the Arab Spring: Politics comes first. *The International Journal of Press/Politics*, 18(2), 115–137.

Wondrak, A. K. (2002). Seen any wildlife? Community conflict and a struggle for the soul of Estes Park, Colorado. *Cultural Geographies*, 9(1), 68–94.

Wood, D. (2007). Iran's strong case for nuclear power is obscured by UN sanctions and geopolitics. *Atoms for Peace: An International Journal*, 1(4), 287–300.

Wood, R. M. (2008). "A hand upon the throat of the nation": Economic sanctions and state repression, 1976–2001. *International Studies Quarterly*, 52(3), 489–513.

Xizhen, Z., & Brown, E. (2000). Policies toward North Korea: A time for new thinking. *Journal of Contemporary China*, 9(25), 535–545.

Yang, J., & Rhee, J. H. (2019). CSR disclosure against boycotts: Evidence from Korea. *Asian Business & Management*. doi:10.1057/s41291-019-00063-5

Zapata Campos, M. J., Hall, C. M., & Backlund, S. (2018). Can MNCs promote more inclusive tourism? Apollo tour operator's sustainability work. *Tourism Geographies*, 20(4), 630–652.

Index

Printed in the United States
by Baker & Taylor Publisher Services